GREYSTONE'S

Creative Hands

EDITOR

Beverley Hilton

GREYSTONE PRESS/NEW YORK · TORONTO · LONDON

Volume 6

Contents

© Fratelli Fabri Editore, Milan 1966, 1967
Marshall Cavendish Limited 1970, 1971, 1972, 1973, 1975
Manufactured in the United States of America
Library of Congress Catalog Card No. 75-8338

Much of the material contained herein has previously been published in separate parts under the title Golden Hands.

Pattern Library

Bird and a flower

This bright-colored design of a bird with outspread wings and a brilliant scarlet flower has a tropical feeling about it and makes an ideal motif for working on canvas or linen. Using 6-strand floss and worked in cross-stitch, the design could be adapted for a beautiful and eye-catching bedspread, the motif repeated on a squared-off background.

The yarn colors suggested for the embroidery are: D.M.C. 6-strand embroidery floss in Geranium 350, Cobalt Blue 797, Grass Green 703, Canary Yellow 973, and the background in White.

551

The hole truth

Unless buttonholes are worked very neatly, they can spoil the appearance of an otherwise perfectly made garment.
Depending on the size of the button and the width of the buttonhole border, one of several different methods can be applied. The holes can be worked horizontally when the buttonhole band is fairly wide, whereas on a narrow band it is neater to work them vertically. Buttonholes on baby garments are worked as eyelet holes.

Horizontal buttonholes

Simple buttonhole
When the buttonhole is to be made as part of the main section of a cardigan, finish at the center front edge. On the next row, work a few stitches to the position for the buttonhole, then bind off the number of stitches needed for the size of the button and work to the end of the row. On the following row, work to the bound-off stitches in the previous row, turn the work and cast on the same number of stitches, turn the work again and continue to the end of the row. Always remember to work the stitch immediately after the last cast-on stitch fairly tightly in order to make the buttonhole look even.

A perfect buttonhole
Often a horizontal cast-on and bound-off buttonhole is spoiled by a loose loop of yarn across one end. To avoid this, work as follows:
Work the first row as given, binding off the full number of stitches. On the second row work to the last stitch before the bound-off stitches and increase in this stitch by working into the front and back of it. Then cast on one stitch fewer than you bound off so that you retain the correct number of stitches.

Tailored buttonhole
When the position for the buttonhole is reached, work the stitches required for the size of the button in a different colored yarn, then slip these stitches back onto the left-hand needle and work them again in the original yarn being used. When the work is finished, pull out the different colored yarn, being careful not to drop the stitches. Now complete the buttonhole by threading a length of the correct yarn through these stitches. Oversew, or buttonhole stitch, around the edges to hold the buttonhole and make it neat.

Vertical buttonholes

Work until the point for the buttonhole is reached. On the next row work a few stitches to the position for the buttonhole, then work the required number of rows over these stitches for the size of the button. Break off the yarn and return to the remaining stitches. Attach the yarn and work the same number of rows over these stitches, then continue across all the stitches in the usual manner.

Layette buttonhole

Work until the point for the buttonhole is reached. On the next row work a few stitches into the position for the buttonhole, pass the yarn over or around the needle to make an eyelet hole and work the next two stitches together. On the next row work across all the stitches in the usual way, including the yarn over stitch.

Reinforcing buttonholes

All buttonholes, except possibly those on baby garments, require reinforcing before they are complete to prevent fraying. Vertical and horizontal buttonholes require buttonhole stitching in matching silk along both edges with one straight stitch and two slanted stitches at each end. Small round eyelets require several evenly spaced buttonhole stitches around the hole, the loops lying toward the center.
Be careful not to work too many stitches around the hole (this would stretch the edges) or too few stitches (this would make the buttonhole smaller than intended).

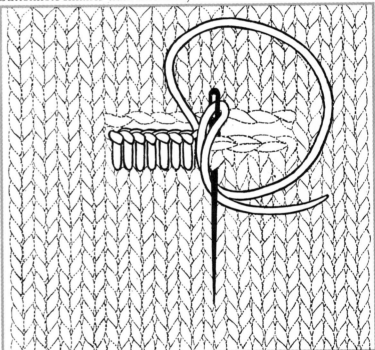

▲ *Working buttonhole stitch to strengthen a knitted buttonhole*
▼ *Correctly reinforced buttonhole with slanted stitches at each end*

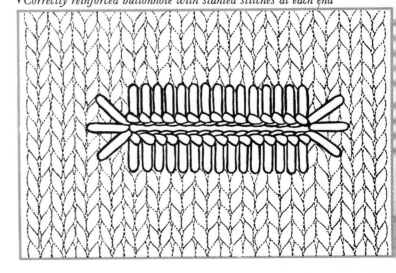

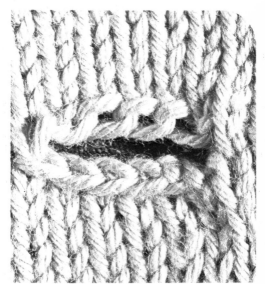

▲ *Simple buttonhole binding off*   ▲ *Simple buttonhole casting on*   ▲ *Simple buttonhole completed*

▲ *Method for tailored buttonhole with contrast yarn used for clarity*

▼ *Vertical buttonhole, one side completed*   ▼ *Layette eyelet buttonhole*

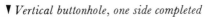

Party looks for mothers-to-be

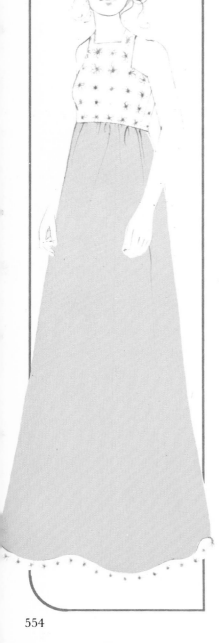

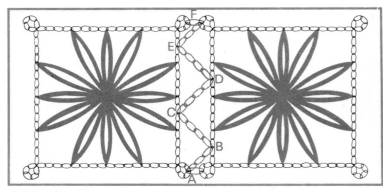

Joining daisy squares by working zigzag chain stitch into edge

Working hundreds of daisies and sewing them together to make fabric is the simplest technique in daisy work. You can get more ambitious results by combining daisies with crochet. Here is a standard method for crocheting daisies together which you can use for the usual twelve-petaled daisy as long as you remember to treat each petal as a single loop, even if it has two or three layers. Note: The Hero Crazy Daisy Winder is available in most needlework departments in 2″ and 3″ sizes.

Crocheting daisies together

Edging the daisy. Work 1ss into tip of first petal, (ch4, 1sc into tip of next petal) twice, *ch9, 1ss into 4th ch to form picot. (Ch4, 1sc into tip of next petal) 3 times. Repeat from * twice more, ch9, 1ss into 4th ch to form picot, ch4, 1sc into first ss at beginning of round. Break yarn and finish off by darning end in on wrong side. This will turn loose daisies into daisy squares, with crocheted edgings and picots at the 4 corners.

Join daisies. Work a zigzag chain between squares, working by turns into each side of the daisy edge. 1ss into picots of both daisies (A), ch3, 1sc into edge of first daisy between first 2 petals (B), ch3, 1sc into edge of second daisy between next 2 petals (C), ch3, 1sc into first daisy edge again (D), ch3, 1sc into second daisy edge again (E), ch3, 1ss into picots

of both daisies (F).
Build a fabric by joining the loose daisy squares with a zig-zag chain.

Daisy-trim a gown

Crochet daisies into a delicate bodice, add a swirl of cool green voile, and more daisies to trim the hem for a really young and pretty evening dress. Scatter a few daisies in your hair to add to the effect, then dance all night and you'll still look cool and fresh in the morning! And, if you're a young mother-to-be, you will find it's the prettiest dress to be pregnant in!

You will need:
N.B. Dress for size 34in bust.
☐ Hero Crazy Daisy Winder (2in diameter)
☐ 5oz 3 ply fingering yarn
☐ 3½yd voile
☐ 4yd fine lawn
☐ 7 button molds to cover— ½in or ⅝in diameter
☐ No.B (2.00 mm) crochet hook
☐ 1 hook and eye, size 3
☐ 1 spool matching thread
☐ 8in skirt zipper

Instructions for making daisy bodice

Make 72 separate daisies (3 windings without lock stitch edging) for the bodice and about 30 for the hem trimming. Crochet the edges for each daisy separately. Crochet daisy squares together for the bodice, starting from the bottom and working upward, making 3 rows of 16 daisies. Then build up back and front as shown. Crochet together at the shoulder seams, then work 7 loops where they are shown in the diagram.
To make a loop, work 1ss into crochet edge of daisy, ch6, anchor with another ss into daisy edge.
Finally, crochet together remaining daisy squares for the hem trimming.

Making the evening dress

Copy the bodice pattern from the graph onto paper. Fold the cotton lawn lengthwise, selvages together, and lay out the pattern as in the diagram with ½in seam allowance. As the

Diagram for building up daisy bodice. Each square represents one daisy

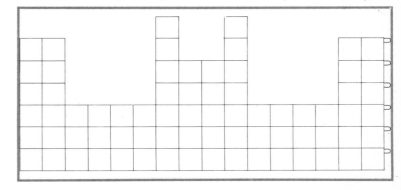

bodice is lined throughout, cut the pattern twice. Using the top layer, pin darts and seams, baste and fit. Transfer alterations to lining.

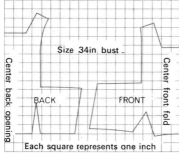

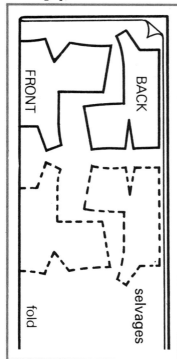

▲ *Bodice graph*

▲ *Layout for 36in wide fabric*

The bodice

Stitch darts and shoulder seams, leaving the side seams open in both top and lining, and press. Lay lining and top fabric together, right sides facing. Pin, baste and stitch along seamlines around neck, down center back and around armholes, finishing 1½in from each side seam. Notch carefully into each corner and pull the bodice inside out by easing the back sections through the shoulder straps. Pin side seams together in each layer and stitch. Press seams open and finish stitching around armhole across side seams. Baste along all seam edges and press them flat.

The skirt and lining

Cut off 9in from the length of voile for facings and covered buttons. Cut remaining voile in half widthwise for front and back of skirt. Fold each length, selvages together, and mark the fold line for center front and center back. On the center back fold, mark 8in from the top edge. This is for the length of the opening.

Cut a strip of voile 8in long and 3in wide and make a placket, finishing the lower end with a tiny bar across the point from the outside to strengthen it. Stitch back and front of skirt together along selvages. Trim and overcast the seam if the selvages are too tight.

Make the lining the same as the top skirt, but this time make a simple faced opening and insert the zipper. To stitch the lining to the skirt, place the corresponding skirt and lining openings together, matching the side seams and center fronts. Pin and baste. Make two rows of gathering stitches along bodice seam ¼in apart.

Attaching skirt to bodice and finishing

Pin the skirt to the outside fabric of the bodice, right sides together, matching edges, seams and center marks. Draw up the gathers, pin, baste and stitch. Press seam toward bodice. Fold the seam allowance on bodice lining to inside and hem to the bodice seamline. This gives a neat finish with no seams showing.

Sew 3 snap fasteners on the skirt opening and a hook and eye on the bodice seam at the top of the zipper on the inside of the skirt. Lay the daisy bodice over the fabric bodice and pin from the corners, allowing the crochet edge to overlap slightly. Draw in the ease along the shoulder edge of the armhole with colored basting thread which can be easily removed afterward. Slip stitch around all edges. Ease the fullness over the darts, leaving it flat at the side seams. Sew on buttons down center back. Turn up the hem, making the lining ½in shorter. Sew the daisy border along the bottom.

Dress-making 28

Basic blouse into shirt

Here is the first of the blouse conversions from the Creative Pattern Pack which was introduced in Dressmaking chapter 1, page 28. It is a traditional fitted shirt with tailored lines and classic good looks.

A special feature of this shirt is the seaming. It is stitched with French seams, a method which gives the seams a neat and durable finish—useful for garments like shirts that have to stand up to frequent laundering.

Another feature of the conversion is the way the cuffs are treated. With this blouse, the sleeves may be finished with single or double cuffs which fasten with link buttoning. Instructions for making the cuffs are in the next chapter, p 576.

The fitted shirt

Suitable fabrics

Plain and printed silk, cotton, linen or light woolen fabrics.

Fabric requirements and notions

☐ 36in wide fabric: for sizes 32½ and 34in, 2⅞ yards; for size 36in, 3 yards; for sizes 38 to 42in, 3⅛ yards.

☐ Interfacing: for all sizes, ⅜ yard. For silk fabric this should be preshrunk lawn; for other fabrics, a fine poplin.

☐ Buttons: 8 for single front buttoning, 12 for buttoning in groups of three. Allow 4 extra for linked button cuffs in both cases.

☐ Matching thread.

The shirt pattern

From the basic blouse pattern you will need pattern pieces 1 and 2, which are the front and back.

From the accessory sheet you will need pattern pieces 8, 10, 11 and 12, which are the shirt sleeve, shirt collar, collarband and cuff patterns.

The shirt also needs a front facing, which you make as follows: Lay the front pattern section on a piece of paper and draw around the shoulder, neck edge, front edge and lower edge. Remove the pattern and make the facing as shown in figure 3. It should be 1½ inches wide at the shoulders and 3 inches wide at the lower edge. Unlike the basic blouse, this shirt is fitted and has back and front body darts. So, if you have made the muslin in Dressmaking chapters 16, page 316 and 17, page 336, copy the darts onto the pattern pieces, otherwise the body darts will be fitted later using the pleat lines as a guide.

Cutting out the shirt

Select the correct layout on page 559, according to your size. Remember that the patterns have no seam allowance, so add ⅝ inch seam and hem allowances all around. The seam allowance is not ¾ inch as for most of the other garments given so far, because less seam allowance is required for French seams.

556

For classic good looks the fitted shirt has few rivals

The following points should be considered.

Decide what sort of cuffs you want. If you want them single (i.e. cuffs half the depth of the cuff pattern, as figure 1), you will only need two cuff pieces. But if you want double cuffs (i.e. cuffs cut to the depth of the cuff pattern, folded over and closed with link buttons, as figure 2), you will need four cuff pieces.

If you have chosen a striped fabric and wish to make a feature of the stripes, copy the other half of the collar pattern and join the two at the center back. When laying out the collar pattern, place the lengthwise grain line on the pattern along the crosswise grain on the fabric.

Cut out the fabric and keep the remnants, as you will need them later.

Mark the pattern details. Pay special attention to the collar and collarband details, the balance marks and the center markings. The collar ends should meet on the center front line, with the ends of the collarband meeting the edges of the shirt front.

To hold in the fullness around the lower edge of the sleeves, you have a choice. If the fabric is soft, disregard the pleat markings,

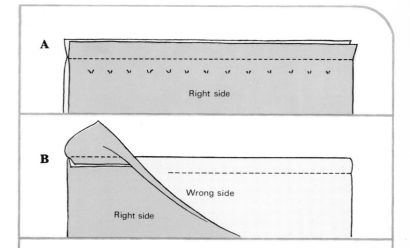

1. ▲ *The single cuff with topstitching detail*

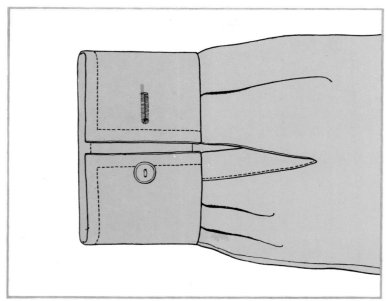

2. ▲ *The double cuff for link buttoning*

as you can simply gather the lower edge to fit the cuff. For crisper and bulkier fabrics, mark the pleat details.
Remove the pattern pieces.

Interfacing
To give the collar and cuffs that extra crispness which is required for a shirt, they should be interfaced.
Cut one collar piece and one collarband from the interfacing with the center back on the fold, as indicated on the layout. If you are making double cuffs, cut two cuff pieces from the interfacing. If the cuffs are to be single, cut two pieces half the depth of the cuffs, as the interfacing needs to go only to the point where the cuffs are folded over.
Pin and baste each interfacing piece to the wrong side of a corresponding shirt piece. The interfacing should go on that piece which will be uppermost.

Fitting
Baste the darts, side and shoulder seams and try on the shirt,

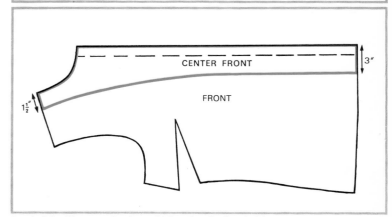

The French seam

The French seam is a double seam with the raw edges encased.
A. With wrong sides facing, first pin and stitch the seam $\frac{3}{8}$ inch from the seamline inside the seam allowance.
Trim and lightly press the stitched seam toward the front. Turn the garment inside out.
B. Working on the wrong side, pin, baste and stitch along the original seamline, encasing the raw edges in the seam.

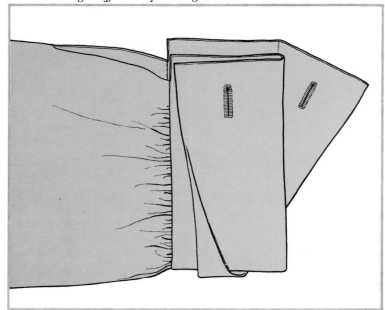

3. ▲ *Marking out the front facing for the fitted shirt*

pinning it together along the center front line. If you have not already marked the body darts on the pattern, extend the pleat lines into darts, running them out smoothly at each end.
Make any alterations necessary, following the fitting instructions for the muslin in Dressmaking chapter 16, page 316.
Try the sleeves for length with the cuffs basted in position.

Making the shirt
With right sides together pin, baste and stitch the facings to the front edges. Do not stitch them along the neck and hem edges. Turn the facings to the inside, edge-baste and press.
Stitch all the darts. Press the side bust darts flat and the underbust and all the back darts toward the center line.
Make French seams, as shown, on the side and shoulder seams. Before making the second row of stitches which encase the raw seam edges, press the edges lightly toward the front and then stitch along the seamline.
Press the finished French seams toward the front.
Turn up the hem as for the blouse in Dressmaking 19, page 368.

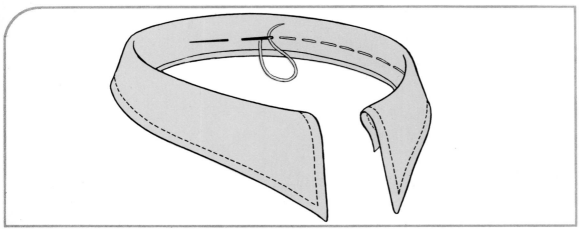

4. ▲ *Rolling the collar and basting along the lower edge*   **5. ▼** *Stitching the collar between the collarbands*

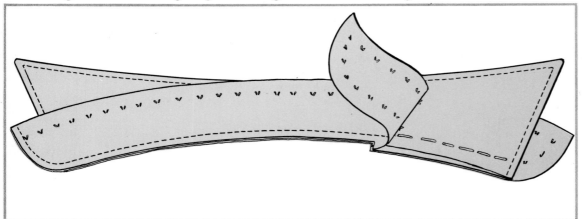

6. ▲ *Basting along the stitched edges of the collarband*   **7. ▼** *Basting the outer collarband over the stitching line*

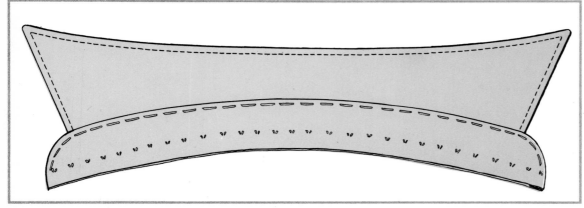

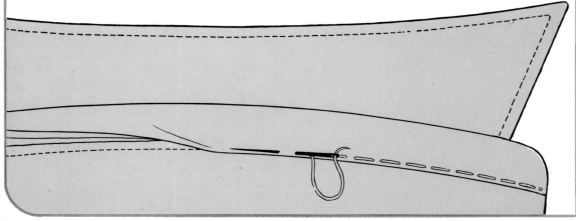

Making the collar

Working on a flat surface, place the top (interfaced) and under collar pieces together, right sides facing. Pin, baste and stitch along the front edges and the upper curved seam.

Trim the seam allowance to $\frac{1}{4}$ inch, trim across the corners and turn to the right side. Baste along the stitched edges and press.

If you want to topstitch the collar do so now, stitching $\frac{1}{4}$ inch from the edge.

Roll the collar in the position you would wear it, as shown in figure 4. You will see that the lower edge of the top collar rises above the edge of the under collar. Baste it firmly in this position along the seamline of the under collar.

To complete the collar, stitch it to the collarband. Matching all markings, place the collar between the inner and outer collarband pieces, as shown in figure 5, and stitch, leaving the lower edge open.

Trim the seam allowance on the stitched edges of the collarband to $\frac{1}{4}$ inch and turn to the right side. Baste along the stitched edges, as shown in figure 6, and press.

The ends of the collarband have now become the tabs for the button and buttonhole. Should you find that the tabs are too bulky, notch the seam allowance, as this will help to flatten them.

Stitching on the collar

Baste the front facing to the shirt along the neckline.

Pin the inner collarband along the inside of the neckline with the raw edges even, carefully matching the balance marks.

Baste, stitch and trim the seam allowance.

Turn under the seam allowance on the outer collarband, lay it over the stitching line to cover the machine stitches, as shown in figure 7. Carefully slip stitch in place.

Be very careful when you hand-sew along the tab, because this part will show when the collar is buttoned.

Layouts for the fitted shirt

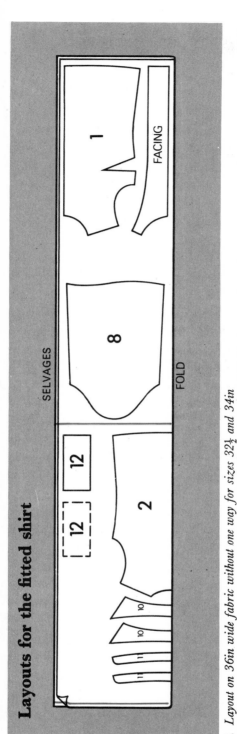

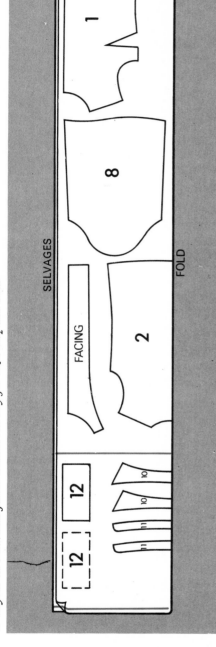

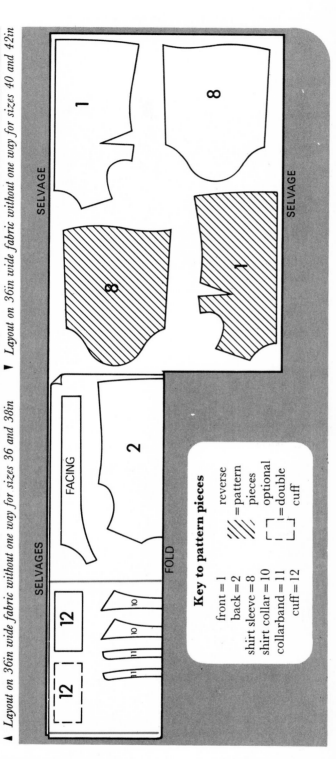

▲ Layout on 36in wide fabric without one way for sizes 32½ and 34in

▲ Layout on 36in wide fabric without one way for sizes 36 and 38in

▼ Layout on 36in wide fabric without one way for sizes 40 and 42in

Key to pattern pieces

front = 1   reverse
back = 2   ⧄ = pattern pieces
shirt sleeve = 8
shirt collar = 10   ⌐⌐ = optional
collarband = 11   ⌐⌐ = double
cuff = 12   cuff

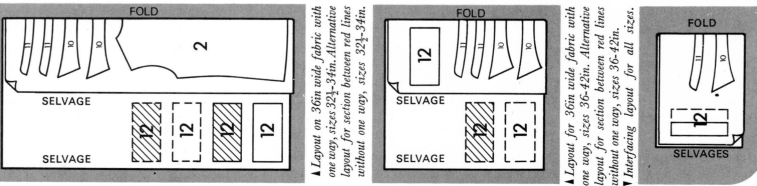

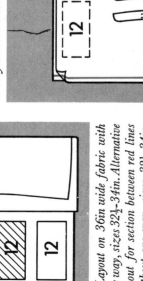

▲ Layout on 36in wide fabric with one way, sizes 32½–34in. Alternative layout for section between red lines without one way, sizes 32½–34in.

▲ Layout on 36in wide fabric with one way, sizes 36–42in. Alternative layout for section between red lines without one way, sizes 36–42in.

▼ Interfacing layout for all sizes.

559

Furnishing Fashion Flair

Design for a magic carpet
Here is the final section of the Numdah rug design—the border and the other center section appeared in the last two Furnishing Fashion Flair chapters, pgs. 520, 540.

Tambour work is recommended for making the rug, using different colored embroidery threads on thick, off-white felt. Instructions for tambour work are given in Embroidery 14, page 268.

The design could also be worked in chain stitch or with machine embroidery. Felt rugs need to be backed only if they are on bare floors, as felt will not slip on a carpet.

Moorish motif in cross-stitch

Pattern Library

This simple geometric design in cross-stitch can be used as a repeating motif, or the individual motifs could be used singly or in groups—work them in a circle for a pillow top or along the flap of a handbag. The needlepoint shown here was worked in tapestry yarn in pink, green and blue, and the background in white. If you copy this design on double-thread canvas with 10 double threads to 1 inch, the area illustrated here will measure, on completion, approximately 2 inches square. Simply repeat this motif to build up an exquisite design for a chair.

Lacy looks in knitting

Knitting Know-how 29

These lacy patterns are worked by putting the yarn over or around the needle to form an eyelet hole and decreasing a stitch at a given point to compensate.

Ivy leaf stitch

Cast on a number of stitches divisible by 10, plus 5.

1st row. Sl 1, K1, *P1, K2, K2 tog, ytf, K1, ytf, sl 1, K1, psso, K2, rep from * ending P1, K2.
2nd row. Sl 1, K1, *K1, P9, rep from * ending K3.
3rd row. Sl 1, K1, *P1, K1, K2 tog, K1, ytf, K1, ytf, K1, sl 1, K1, psso, K1, rep from * ending P1, K2.
4th row. As 2nd.
5th row. Sl 1, K1, *P1, K2 tog, K2, ytf, K1, ytf, K2, sl 1, K1, psso, rep from * ending P1, K2.
6th row. As 2nd.
7th row. Sl 1, K1, *K1, ytf, sl 1, K1, psso, K2, P1, K2, K2 tog, ytf, rep from * ending K3.
8th row. Sl 1, K1, *P5, K1, P4, rep from * ending P1, K2.
9th row. Sl 1, K1, *K1, ytf, K1, sl 1, K1, psso, K1, P1, K1, K2 tog, K1, ytf, rep from * ending K3.
10th row. As 8th.
11th row. Sl 1, K1, *K1, ytf, K2, sl 1, K1, psso, P1, K2 tog, K2, ytf, rep from * ending K3.
12th row. As 8th.
These 12 rows form pattern and are repeated throughout.

Broken lace rib stitch

Cast on a number of stitches divisible by 7, plus 6.

1st row. Sl 1, K1, * P2, ytf, sl 1, K1, psso, K1, K2 tog, yrn, rep from * ending P2, K2.
2nd row. Sl 1, K1, *K2, P5, rep from * ending K4.
Repeat 1st and 2nd rows twice more.
7th row. Sl 1, K1, *P2, K5, rep from * ending P2, K2.
8th row. As 2nd.
9th row. Sl 1, K1, *P2, K2 tog, ytf, K1, ytf, sl 1, K1, psso, rep from * ending P2, K2.
10th row. As 2nd.
Repeat 9th and 10th rows twice more.
15th row. As 7th.
16th row. As 2nd.
These 16 rows form pattern and are repeated throughout.

Bramble stitch

Cast on a number of stitches divisible by 4, plus 4.

1st row (wrong side). Sl 1, K1, *P3 tog into next st K1, P1, K1, rep from * ending K2.
2nd row. Sl 1, K1, P to last 2 sts, K2.

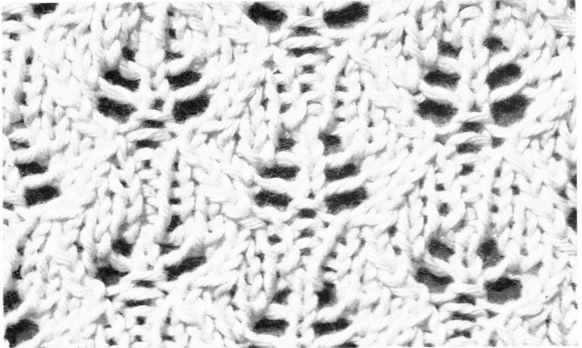

▲ *Ivy leaf stitch*

▼ *Broken lace rib stitch*

562

3rd row. Sl 1, K1 *into next st K1, P1, K1, P3 tog, rep from * ending K2.
4th row. As 2nd.
These 4 rows form pattern and are repeated throughout.

Window pane stitch

Cast on a number of stitches divisible by 12, plus 7.
1st row. Sl 1, K1, *P3, K3, ytf, sl 1, K2 tog, psso, ytf, K3, rep from * ending P3, K2.
2nd row. Sl 1, K1, *K3, P9, rep from * ending K5.
3rd row. Sl 1, K1, *P3, K1, K2 tog, ytf, K3, ytf, sl 1, K1, psso, K1, rep from * ending P3, K2.
4th row. As 2nd.
Repeat 1st-4th rows twice more.
13th row. Sl 1, K1, *ytf, sl 1, K2 tog, psso, ytf, K3, P3, K3, rep from * ending ytf, sl 1, K2 tog, psso, ytf, K2.
14th row. Sl 1, K1, *P6, K3, P3, rep from * ending P3, K2.
15th row. Sl 1, K1, *K3, ytf, sl 1, K1, psso, K1, P3, K1, K2 tog, ytf, rep from * ending K5.
16th row. As 14th.
Repeat 13th-16th rows twice more.
These 24 rows form pattern and are repeated throughout.

Eyelet rib stitch

Cast on a number of stitches divisible by 14, plus 4.
1st row. Sl 1, K1, *P2, K3 tbl, P2, rep from * ending K2.
2nd row. Sl 1, K1, *K2, P3 tbl, K2, rep from * ending K2.
3rd row. Sl 1, K1, *P2, ytf, sl 1, K2 tog, psso, yrn, P4, K3 tbl, P2, rep from * ending K2.
4th row. Sl 1, K1, *K2, P3 tbl, K4, P1, P1 tbl, P1, K2, rep from * ending K2.
5th row. As 1st.
6th row. As 2nd.
7th row. Sl 1, K1, *P2, K3 tbl, P4, ytf, sl 1, K2 tog, psso, yrn, P2, rep from * ending K2.
8th row. Sl 1, K1, *K2, P1, P1 tbl, P1, K4, P3 tbl, K2, rep from * ending K2.
These 8 rows form pattern and are repeated throughout.

▲ *Bramble stitch*

▼ *Window pane stitch*

▼ *Eyelet rib stitch*

Basic Wardrobe Knitting

Anyone for tennis?

These neatly tailored sweaters, the sports cardigan and pullover featured in the illustration below, are designed to be worn by either a man or a woman and the instructions are given in a wide size range, from 34 inch bust to 44 inch chest. The contrasting color band on the front of the cardigan is worked after the garment is completed, so that the buttonholes can be worked on either the left or the right side. The cardigan has a single cable panel on both fronts, while the pullover is worked in a cable and rib pattern. Work the contrasting stripes in blue and red, your own club or school colors, or substitute white yarn for the contrast if you prefer.

Cardigan for a man or a woman

Sizes

Directions are for 34in bust or chest.
The figures in brackets [] refer to the 36, 38, 40, 42 and 44in sizes respectively.
Length down center back, 24½[24¾:25¼:27½:28:28¼]in.
Sleeve seam, 17½[17½:18:18:19:19]in, adjustable.

Gauge

6sts and 8 rows to 1in over stockinette stitch worked on No.5 needles.

Materials

Reynolds Classique (50-gram balls)
5[6:6:6:7:7] balls of main color A
1 ball of contrast B
1 ball of contrast C
One pair of No.4 needles (or Canadian No.9)
One pair of No.5 needles (or Canadian No.8)
One cable needle
Four buttons

Back

Using No.4 needles and color A, cast on 98[106:110:118:122:130] sts.
1st row K2, *P2, K2, rep from * to end.
2nd row P2, *K2, P2, rep from * to end.
Rep 1st and 2nd rows until work measures 3[3:3:3½:3½:3½]in, dec one st at each end of last row on 36, 40 and 44in sizes only. 98[104:110:116:122:128] sts.
Change to No.5 needles and st st, beg with a K row. Continue in st st, inc one st at each end of 19th and every 18th[18th:18th:20th:20th:20th] row until there are 108 [114:120:126:132:138] sts.
Continue without shaping until work measures 16[16:16:18:18:18]in, ending with a WS row.

Shape armholes

Bind off 1[2:2:3:3:4] sts at beg of next 2 rows.
3rd row K2, sl 1 knitwise, K1, psso, K to last 4sts, K2 tog, K2.
4th row P.
Rep last 2 rows 10[11:12:13:14:15] times more.
Work 22 rows without shaping.

Shape shoulders

1st row K3, sl 1 knitwise, K1, psso, K to last 5sts, K2 tog, K3.
2nd row P3, P2 tog, P to last 5sts, P2 tog tbl, P3.
Rep last 2 rows 11[11:12:12:13:13] times more.
Bind off rem 36[38:38:40:40:42] sts.

Left front

Using No.4 needles and color A, cast on 42[45:48:51:54:57] sts.
1st row K2[K1:0:P1, K2:K2:K1], *P2, K2, rep from * to end.
2nd row *P2, K2, rep from

Cable stitch detail of front panel of cardigan

Continental shaped sleeves for freedom of movement

* to last 2[1:0:3:2:1] sts, P2 [P1:0:P2, K1:P2:P1].

Rep 1st and 2nd rows until work measures 3[3:3:3½:3½: 3½]in.

Change to No.5 needles and cable patt.

1st patt row K17[19:21:23: 25:27] sts, P2, K6, P2, K15 [16:17:18:19:20] sts.

2nd patt row P15[16:17:18: 19:20] sts, K2, P6, K2, P17 [19:21:23:25:27] sts.

Rep 1st and 2nd patt rows 7 times more.

17th patt row K17[19:21: 23:25:27] sts, P2, sl next 3sts on cable needle and hold at back of work, K next 3sts,

K3 from cable needle—called C6B—P2, K to end.

18th patt row As 2nd patt row. These 18 rows form the cable patt and are rep throughout left front. Continue in patt, inc one st at side edge of next row, then every 18th[18th:18th:20th: 20th:20th] row until there are 47[50:53:56:59:62] sts. Continue without shaping until work measures same as back to armhole ending at side edge.

Shape armhole and front
1st row Bind off 1[2:2:3:3:4] sts, patt to last 4sts, K2 tog,

K2.

2nd row Patt to end.

3rd row K2, sl 1 knitwise, K1, psso, patt to end.

4th row Patt to end.

Continue dec at armhole edge on next 10[11:12:13:14:15] RS rows and at center front edge on next row, then every 4th row until 24[24:26:26:28: 28] sts rem.

Continue without shaping until armhole measures same as back to shoulder, ending at armhole edge.

Shape shoulder
1st row K3, sl 1 knitwise, K1, psso, patt to end.

2nd row Patt to last 5sts, P2 tog tbl, P3.

Rep 1st and 2nd rows until 4sts rem.

Dec one st at neck edge until all sts have been worked off. Fasten off.

Right front

Using No.4 needles and color A, cast on 42[45:48:51:54:57] sts.

1st row *K2, P2, rep from * to last 2[1:0:3:2:1] sts, K2[K1:0:P1, K2:K3:K1].

2nd row P2[P1:0:P2, K1: P2:P1], *K2, P2, rep from * to end.

Rep 1st and 2nd rows until work measures 3[3:3:3½:3½:3½]in.

Change to No.5 needles and cable patt.

1st patt row K15[16:17:18:19:20] sts, P2, K6, P2, K17 [19:21:23:25:27] sts.

2nd patt row P17[19:21:23:25:27] sts, K2, P6, K2, P15[16:17:18:19:20] sts.

Rep 1st and 2nd patt rows 7 times more.

17th patt row K15[16:17:18:19:20] sts, P2, C6B, P2, K to end.

18th patt row As 2nd patt row. These 18 rows form the cable patt and are rep throughout the right front.

Continue in patt, inc one st at side edge on next row, then every 18th[18th:18th:20th:20th:20th] row until there are 47[50:53:56:59:62] sts.

Continue without shaping until work measures same as back to armhole, ending at front edge.

Shape armhole and front

1st row K2, sl 1 knitwise, K1, psso, patt to end.

2nd row Bind off 1[2:2:3:3:4] sts, patt to end.

3rd row Patt to last 4sts, K2 tog, K2.

4th row Patt to end.

Complete as given for left front, reversing shaping.

Sleeves

Using No.4 needles and color A, cast on 44[44:48:48:52:52] sts.

1st row *K2, P2, rep from * to end.

Rep 1st row until work measures 3[3:3:3½:3½:3½]in.

Change to No.5 needles and st st, beg with a K row.

Continue in st st, inc one st at each end of next and every 8th row until there are 72[76:78:82:84:88] sts.

Continue without shaping until sleeve measures 17½ [17½:18:18:19:19]in or required length, ending with a WS row.

Shape cap

Bind off 1[2:2:3:3:4] sts at beg of next 2 rows.

Work 2 rows.

5th row K2, sl 1 knitwise, K1, psso, K to last 4sts, K2 tog, K2.

6th row P.

7th row K.

8th row P.

Rep last 4 rows once more.

Rep 5th and 6th rows 10[11:12:13:14:15] times.

Next row K2, sl 1 knitwise, K1, psso, K to last 4sts, K2 tog, K2.

Next row P2, P2 tog, P to last 4sts, P2 tog tbl, P2.

Rep last 2 rows until 24sts rem.

Rep 5th-8th rows until 12 sts rem.

Work 3[3:5:5:7:7] rows. Bind off.

Finishing

Press all pieces under a damp cloth with a warm iron, excluding ribbing.

Sew sleeves into armholes matching cap of sleeves to bound-off edges.

Using No.4 needles and color B, with RS of front facing, pick up and K156[158:160:176:178:180] sts from cast-on edge to shoulder seam, pick up and K60[62:62:64:64:66] sts evenly around sleeve caps and back, pick up and K156[158:160:160:176:178:180] sts down other front. Work 3 rows K1, P1 rib with B, 4 rows with A and 4 rows with C. Mark positions for 4 buttons and work buttonholes on next row by binding off 3sts for each buttonhole on right front for her and left front for him. On following row cast on 3sts over bound-off sts of previous row. Work 2 rows more with C. Bind off in rib. Join side and sleeve seams. Sew on buttons.

Pullover for a man or a woman

Sizes

Directions are for 34in bust or chest.

The figures in brackets [] refer to the 36, 38, 40, 42 and 44in sizes respectively.

Length to shoulder, 21½ [21¾:22:25¼:25½:25¾]in.

Sleeve seam, 17[17:17½:18:18:19]in.

Gauge

8sts and 10 rows to 1in over stockinette stitch worked on No.3 needles.

Materials

3-ply Fingering Yarn (1oz skeins)

13[14:14:16:16:17] skeins of main color A

1 skein of contrast B

1 skein of contrast C

One pair No.2 needles (or Canadian No.11)

One pair No.3 needles (or Canadian No.10)

One cable needle

Back

Using No.2 needles and color A, cast on 156[164:172:180:188:196] sts.

Work 3[3:3:3½:3½:3½]in K2, P2 rib.

Change to No.3 needles and st st, beg with a K row.

Work 4 rows C. Break C and leave end for darning in.

Work 4 rows B. Break B and leave end for darning in.

Continue in cable rib using A only.

1st row K2[K6:K10:P4, K10:K4, P4, K10:K8, P4, K10], *P4, K9, P4, K10, rep from * to last 19[23:0:4:8:12] sts, P4, K9, P4, K2[P4, K9, P4, K6:0:P4:P4, K4:P4, K8].

2nd row P2[P6:P10:K4, P10:P4, K4, P10:P8, K4, P10], *K4, P9, K4, P10, rep from * to last 19[23:0:4:8:12] sts, K4, P9, K4, P2[K4, P9, K4, P6:0:K4:K4, P4:K4, P8].

Work 24 more rows in rib, as set.

27th row K2[K6:K10:P4, K10:K4, P4, K10:K8, P4, K10], *P4, K9, P4, cable 10 (to cable 10, slip next 5sts onto cable needle and hold at front of work, K next 5sts, K5 from cable needle), rep from * to last 19[23:0:4:8:12] sts, P4, K9, P4, K2[P4, K9, P4, K6:0:P4:P4, K4:P4, K8].

28th row As 2nd.

These 28 rows form patt and are rep throughout.

Work until 15[15:15:18:18:18]in, ending with a WS row.

Shape armholes

Bind off 4[5:6:7:8:9] sts at beg of next 2 rows.

Dec one st at each end of every RS row 12[13:14:15:16:17] times. 124[128:132:136:140:144] sts.

Work without shaping until armholes measure 6½[6¾:7:7¼:7½:7¾]in, ending with a WS row.

Shape neck and shoulders

1st row Patt 53[54:55:56:57:58] sts, bind off 18[20:22:24:26:28] sts, patt 53[54:55:56:57:58] sts.

Complete left shoulder first.

** Dec one st at neck edge on next 10 rows. Bind off. **

With WS of work facing, attach yarn to rem sts and complete as for left shoulder from ** to **.

Front

Work as given for back until 2 rows less to armhole, ending with a WS row.

Divide for neck

1st row Patt 78[82:86:90:94:98] sts, turn.

Complete left shoulder on these sts.

Work 1 row.

3rd row Bind off 4[5:6:7:8:9] sts, patt to last 2sts, dec one st. Work 1 row.

**Dec one st at each end of every RS row 12[13:14:15:16:17] times, then at center front edge only on every RS row 6[7:8:9:10:11] times.

Work until armhole measures same as back to shoulder. Bind off. **

With RS of work facing, attach yarn to rem sts and patt to end of row.

Next row Bind off 4[5:6:7:8:9] sts, patt to end.

Complete as given for left shoulder from ** to **.

Sleeves

Using No.2 needles and color A, cast on 78[82:86:90:94:98]

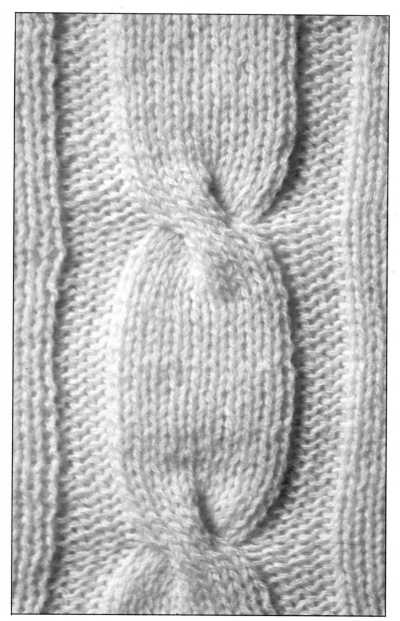

Stitch detail from the pullover

The sleeve length is adjustable on both the pullover and the cardigan

sts.

1st row K2, *P2, K2, rep from * to end.

2nd row P2, *K2, P2, rep from * to end.

Rep 1st and 2nd rows until work measures 3[3:3:3½: 3½:3½]in, ending with a WS row.

Change to No.3 needles and st st, beg with a K row.

Work 4 rows C and 4 rows B. Continue with A only in rib patt.

1st row K3[5:7:9:P2, K9: P4, K9], P4, K10, P4, *K9, P4, K10, P4, rep from * to last 3[5:7:9:11:13] sts, K3[5:7:9:K9, P2:K9, P4]. Continue in rib as given for

back, working cables on 27th and every following 28th row; *at the same time* inc one st at each end of 3rd and every 6th[6th:5th:5th: 5th:5th] row until there are 118[124:130:136:142:148] sts. Continue without shaping until sleeve measures 17[17: 17½:18:18:19]in or required length, ending with a WS row.

Shape cap

Bind off 4[5:6:7:8:9] sts at beg of next 2 rows.

Dec one st at each end of every RS row 12[13:14:15: 16:17] times.

Bind off rem sts.

Neckband

Press all pieces lightly under a damp cloth with a warm iron, excluding ribbing. Join left shoulder seam. Using No.2 needles and B, with RS facing, pick up and K44[46: 48:50:52:54] sts evenly around back neck to left shoulder seam, pick up and K64[66: 68:70:72:74] sts down left front, lift center front thread between right and left front and K center st into back of this thread, pick up and K64 [66:68:70:72:74] sts up right side of front. 173[179:185: 191:197:203] sts.

1st row Work in K1, P1

rib to 2sts before center front st, P2 tog tbl, K1, P2 tog, rib to end.

2nd row Rib to 2sts before center st, K2 tog, P1, K2 tog tbl, rib to end.

Rep 1st and 2nd rows working 1 more row with B, 4 rows with C and 6 rows with A. Bind off. For best results, use the invisible binding-off method given in Knitting Know-how chapter 6.

Finishing

Join bound-off edge of sleeves to straight section of armholes. Sew in remainder of sleeves. Sew side and sleeve seams.

Center pieces in crochet

These crocheted rounds are worked in fine cotton yarn and make pretty center pieces. The center piece with ovals, worked to eleven inches diameter, would also make a useful place mat, but remember that as it will not be heat resistant on a polished table, a protective mat is needed too.

Materials

Center piece with ovals 1 ball J. & P. Coats Knit Cro-Sheen for mat measuring 9in diameter, or 2 balls Coats & Clark's O.N.T. Pearl Cotton for mat measuring 11in diameter. One No.B (2.00 mm) crochet hook.

Center piece with crossed doubles 1 ball Coats & Clark's O.N.T. Speed Cro-Sheen for mat measuring 6in diameter. One No.D (3.00 mm) crochet hook.

Center piece with ovals

Using No.B crochet hook, ch5. Join into a circle with ss. Mark beg of round with colored thread.

1st round Work 10sc into circle. Join with ss to first sc.

2nd round Work 2sc into each sc to end. Join with ss to first sc. 20sc.

3rd round Work in sc to end. Join with ss to first sc.

4th round Work 2sc into each sc to end. Join with ss to first sc. 40sc.

Center piece with ovals can be made in 9in or 11in diameter

5th round As 3rd round.

6th round *Work 1sc into each of next 3sc, 2sc into next sc, rep from * to end. Join with ss to first sc. 50sc.

7th round *5sc, ch1, 1sc into 5th of first 5sc, rep from * ending with ch1, 1sc, when circle will be divided into 10 sections. Join with ss to first sc.

Commence ovals, as follows:

8th round *Ch10, close into a ring with ss into first ch worked, keeping RS facing work 15sc into 10ch ring ending with ss into ch1 space of previous round, work 5sc then ss into next ch1 space on previous round, rep from * ending with ss into base of first oval. 10 ovals formed. Break yarn and fasten off.

9th round Attach yarn in 3rd sc of group of 5sc between 2 ovals of previous round, insert hook in same place and work ch3, *hook into 3rd sc of oval and work 10sc around the oval, 1dc into 3rd sc of group of 5sc between 2 ovals of previous round, rep from * to end. Join with ss to 3rd of first 3ch.

10th round Ch8, *skip 3sc on ring, work 1sc into each of next 4sc of previous round, ch3, 1tr into 1dc, ch3, rep from * to end. Join with ss to 4th of first 8ch.

11th round Ch1, *3sc into ch3 loop of previous round, 3sc into next 3sc of ring, 3sc into next ch3 loop, ch1, rep from * ending with 3sc in 3ch loop.

12th round 1sc into ch1 of previous round, ch1 and 1sc into same place, *skip 1sc, 1sc into each of next 8sc, into next ch1 space work 1sc, ch1, 1sc, rep from * to end.

13th round *Into ch1 space of previous round work 1sc, ch2, 1sc, skip 1sc, 1sc into each of next 9sc, rep from * to end. Join with ss.

14th round Work 1sc, ch2, 1sc into same place as ss, *skip 1sc, 1sc into each of next 5sc, ch2 and 1sc into last of 5sc just worked, skip 1sc, 1sc into each of next 5sc, work 1sc, ch2, 1sc into ch2 space of previous round, rep from * to end. Join with ss into first ch2 space.

15th round Ch8, skip 5sc of previous round, work 1sc into ch2 loop of previous round, *ch7, 1sc into next ch2 loop, rep from * to end. Join with ss to beg of first loop.

16th round *Into ch7 loop work 8sc, ch1, rep from * to end.

17th round *Work 1sc into each of next 8sc, ch1, rep from * to end.

18th round As 17th round, ending with ch2.

19th round *Work 1sc into each of next 8sc, ch2, rep from * ending with 8sc after last rep.

20th round *Ss into ch2 space of previous round, ch12 and close into a ring with ss into first ch, keeping RS facing work 20sc into ring and ss into ch2 space, 1sc into each of next 8sc, rep from * to end to make a total of 20 rings, ending with ss into next st. Break yarn and fasten off.

21st round Attach yarn to 5th sc of group of 8sc between 2 rings, work ch4, hook into 4th sc of ring, *work 13sc around ring, ch1, 1dc into 5th sc of group of 8sc between rings, ch3, 1dc into same sc, ch1, rep from * ending with 1dc into same sc as ch4. Join with ss to 3rd of first 4ch.

22nd round Ch6, *beg in 4th sc of ring work 7sc, ch2, into ch3 space between 2dc of previous round work 1tr, ch2 and 1tr, ch2, rep from * to end. Join with ss to 4th of first 6ch.

23rd round 1sc into next space, *skip first sc of 7sc on ring, 1sc into each of next 6sc on ring, 1sc into next space, 2sc into space between tr, 1sc into next space, rep from * to end. Join with ss to first sc.

24th round 1sc into same place as ss of previous round, 1sc into each of next 3sc, *ch2, skip 1sc, 1sc into each of next 4sc, ch2, skip 1sc, 1sc over center of tr, 1sc into each of next 4sc, rep from * ending with ch2. Join with ss into first sc.

25th round *Skip 1sc, 1sc into each of next 3sc, 1sc into ch2 space of previous round, ch2, 1sc into same space, rep from * to end. Join with ss into next sc.

26th round Ss to center of next ch2 loop, 1sc into same space, *ch7,

Center piece with crossed doubles—for a larger mat, work the pattern in soft knitting cotton, using No.G crochet hook

1sc into ch2 space, rep from * to end. Join with ss to first sc.

27th round *Work 4sc into ch7 loop, ch3 closed to form a picot, 4sc into same loop, rep from * to end. Join with ss. Fasten off.

Center piece with crossed doubles

Using No.D crochet hook, ch5. Join into a circle with ss.

1st round Work 10sc into circle. Join with ss to first sc.

2nd round *Work 1sc into next sc, 2sc into next sc, rep from * to end. Join with ss to first sc. 15sc.

3rd round *Work 1sc into next 2sc, 2sc into next sc, rep from * to end. Join with ss to first sc. 20sc.

4th round *Work 1sc into next sc, 2sc into next sc, rep from * to end. Join with ss to first sc. 30sc.

5th round *Work 1sc into next 5sc, 2sc into next sc, rep from * to end. Join with ss to first sc. 35sc.

6th round Ch5 to count as first dc, 1dc into st before ch5, ch1, *skip 1sc, 1dc into next sc, 1dc into skipped sc, ch1, rep from * to end. Join with ss into top of first 5ch.

7th round 1sc into space between first crossed dc, *ch5, 1sc into space between next crossed dc, rep from * to end. Join with ss to first sc.

8th round Ch1, *into ch5 loop work 3sc, ch1, rep from * to end. Join with ss to first 1ch.

9th round Ch1, work in sc to end working 1sc into each sc and 1sc into ch1 space of previous round. Join with ss to first 1ch.

10th round *Work 1sc into next 4sc, 2sc into next sc, rep from * to end. Join with ss to first sc. 83sc.

11th round Ch6, go back 2sts and into 2nd st work 1dc, ch2, work forward and *skip 2sc, work 1dc into next sc, ch2, work 1dc into first skipped sc, ch2, rep from * to end. Join with ss to 4th of first 6ch.

12th round 1sc into first ch2 space, ch5, *1sc into ch2 between crossed dc of previous row, ch5, rep from * to end. Join with ss to first sc.

13th round Ch1, *3sc into ch5 loop, ch2, rep from * to end. Join with ss to first sc.

14th round Work 1sc and ch1 between one st and the next to end. Fasten off.

Finishing

Place a clean piece of paper on a flat board. Draw out the shape of the mat to the correct measurements. Dip the mat in a weak starch solution, gently squeeze and place on paper. Pin out to shape, using rust-proof pins. When the mat is dry, remove pins. When pinning out loops, make sure the pin is in the center of the loop. Pull out all picots to shape and keep scallops regular.

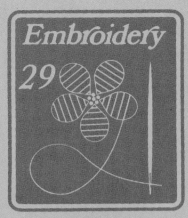

The languid lion

A charming, flower-loving lion to appliqué.

Materials

To make a picture 12 inches wide by 10 inches deep, you will need:

☐ Scraps of russet-colored corduroy
☐ Scraps of pink and green felt
☐ Purple felt, 14 inches wide by 12 inches deep
☐ Sewing thread to match corduroy
☐ Wool yarn, black and russet
☐ 6-strand embroidery floss, yellow, black, green and russet
☐ Piece of hardboard, 12 inches by 10 inches
☐ White glue

Preparing for appliqué

There are eleven pattern pieces in the lion's body: the main body, back leg and tail, two front paws, one back paw, chin, two cheeks, the nose and two ears. Each piece is marked with the grain line and numbered according to the order in which the pieces are to be stitched into position.

Trace each outline separately onto paper, mark the grain lines, and cut out.

Pin each piece of the pattern on the corduroy, matching the grain line to the ridges of the fabric. Cut out each shape, leaving $\frac{1}{4}$-inch turnings all around. Fold the turnings to the back of the fabric and baste, except those edges which are marked on the diagram with a red line. These seam allowances are left flat, the next section being placed on top.

Place the pieces on the purple felt background in the order indicated by the numbers on each piece in the diagram—the main body piece, for instance, is marked number one and so are the ears and nose. Baste and sew each piece into position separately, using backstitch or slip stitch. Work the tail and the mane in long straight stitches using russet yarn and then finish the end of the tail and the edge of the mane with long stitches, using matching floss.

Embroider the eyes, the nose, jawline and claws in satin stitch using black and yellow yarn. French knots are used for the whiskers and backstitch for the outline of the tail, worked in black floss. Embroider the stems of the plants in green, using stem stitch or chain stitch. Cut out the pink flowers and green leaves from felt and fix them to the background, using just a touch of glue.

When the lion is completed, mount the picture on hardboard and then frame.

A clever use of corduroy to achieve a three-dimensional effect

Diagram of pattern showing eleven pieces marked with grain of fabric ►

PLACE ON STRAIGHT GRAIN OF FABRIC

Painting with patches

Patchwork is not just a way of using up old scraps of material; it is an art form in itself. Careful and imaginative use of color and texture can make a piece of patchwork as exciting and varied as a painting, whether you work with templates or "crazy" shapes.

Principles of color

Since color plays such an important part in the design of patchwork, it is a help to understand the principles of color relationship.

Red, yellow and blue are the primary colors from which all other colors are combined.

Secondary colors are made by mixing primary colors. For example, if blue and yellow are mixed in equal parts, the resulting color is green and variations of green can be achieved according to the balance of the primary colors. The tone of a color is its lightness or darkness.

Using color

Before planning a design, consider all the factors involved. For example, if you are making a pillow top, look at all the colors in the room—the carpet, curtains, walls and upholstery. If all or most of these are patterned, it is a good idea to use plain materials in your patchwork. If the room is full of different colors, then pick out the most striking of these and use shades of them in your design. If you have only one main color in your room, then use a contrasting color to make a striking focal point. Closely related colors can make a very effective design. By using, for instance, blue and green only, you will have all the tones of blue from pale blue to navy and all the tones of green, plus the turquoise colors made from mixing blue and green together.

If you prefer to use contrasting colors, keep to one dominant color, one less dominant color and one or two accent colors. For example, if your main color is pink and you wish to use tan as a second, less dominant color, then small quantities of yellow and charcoal used as accent colors will help to co-ordinate the design. Accent colors often look best if they are combined in a patterned patch as shown in figure **1**.

If, however, the only materials available make a jumble of different colors, then pick out and use those featuring the dominant one which will help to give the design some shape. Unless the color demands it, try not to mix naturalistic and abstract patterns because they do not combine well.

Using texture

Patchwork is very effective when textures are mixed (see figure **2**).

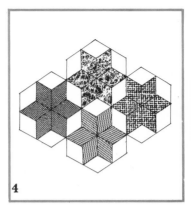

Although it is inadvisable to mix materials of different weights in patchwork which will receive a lot of wear, it is possible to do this with textured patchwork which is intended to be more decorative than hard-wearing. If some of the patches are very lightweight, you can use a bonded fiber fabric lining (see Patchwork chapter 1, page 332).

The texture of a material often alters its color. For example, a patch in red velvet will look glowing and jewel-like, whereas a patch in exactly the same color, but in a shiny material, will seem much lighter and brighter. Mixing silks, velvet, corduroy, satin, nubby tweed and corded silk in approximately the same colors can make a very exciting design.

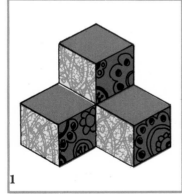

Textural patchwork works best when you limit the number of colors you use and let the structure of the materials create the interest (see figures **3** and **4**).

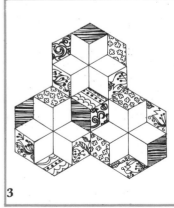

Three-dimensional patchwork

Color alone can be very exciting when it is used to create a three-dimensional effect. Sets of three diamonds joined together can be made to look like boxes piled on top of one another. Use the different patterns and colors as light and shade, highlighting the tops of the boxes and shading the sides (see figure **5**).

Four triangles meeting in a point in the middle and adding up to a square, as shown in figure **6**, can be highlighted on one side more strongly than the other and so make the surface look as though it is coming toward you in points.

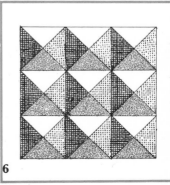

Crazy patchwork

As the picture shows, this is patchwork built up in a truly random way, not only by the use of different materials but also by the total irregularity of the shapes. In many ways this technique is closer to appliqué than patchwork, since the different patches are stitched to a background material and not to each other—the raw edges are turned under and the patches pinned behind each other onto the background. No papers are used for this method.

The advantage of crazy patchwork is that you can use any leftover scraps of material which are too small to be used up in a geometric design.

To make crazy patchwork more interesting, some of the patches can be outlined with embroidery in silk or metallic thread. Little sequins or pearls sewn into the center of a patch, or a cluster of beads on a rather plain material, also add life and variety to the work.

Rich crazy patchwork quilt ►
▼ *Detail of crazy patchwork*

What knots?

The choice of thread thickness in tatting is often governed by the amount which can be carried on the shuttle. Flower motifs such as the six-petaled flower in this chapter can vary considerably both in size and appearance if they are made in different types of thread.

However, if you want to make this six-petaled flower in anything coarser than a soft knitting cotton (such as dishcloth cotton), you will probably have to make a joining in the thread. It is unfortunately not always possible to complete a piece of work without joining two ends of thread together. To avoid spoiling the look of a delicate piece of tatting, it is very important to learn the correct method of joining, so follow the diagrams and instructions carefully.

To join two ends of thread

Joining without a knot
This is the best method. Leave enough of the old thread to wind around the hand, and wind the new thread around with the old to overlap. Work several knots with the double thickness of thread, then drop the old thread and continue with the new. Cut away the ends afterward. Do not use double threads for picots.

Joining with a weaver's knot
Only use this method of joining in the middle of the work if you have made a mistake and have not been able to plan ahead for joining without a knot. However, you can knot the ends at the beginning or end of a ring or chain and sew them in invisibly afterward.

Hold the two ends firmly crossed, left over right, with the index finger and thumb of the left hand.

With the right hand, pass the underneath thread over the thumb of the left hand to form a ring and through, between the two ends. Again with the right hand, take the end of the other thread and insert it downward through the ring.

Take the two ends and draw them upward with the right hand to tighten.

To make the 6-petaled flower

Start with a ring of 8ds, 1p, 8ds, 1p, 8ds, 1p, 8ds, close. Do not leave space but make another ring: *8ds, join to third picot of previous ring, 8ds, 1p, 8ds, 1p, 8ds, close*.

Repeat from * to * and continue in this way until 6 rings have been made, joining the last ring to the first p of the first ring, 8ds. Tie and cut.

A series of motifs can be joined together by the outer picots. You can make other attractive motifs based upon the 6-petaled flower by varying the numbers of picots and double knots.

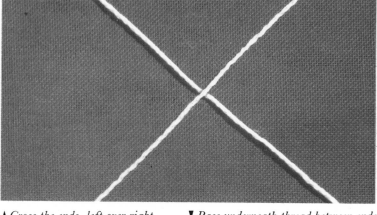

▲ *Cross the ends, left over right*   ▼ *Pass underneath thread between ends*

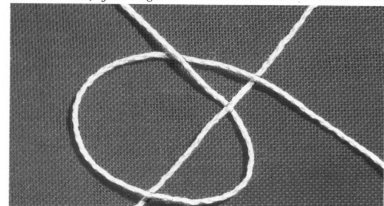

▼ *The end of the other thread is inserted downward through the ring*

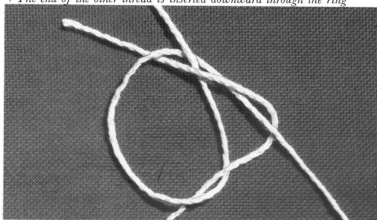

▼ *Finally the two ends are drawn up tight, forming a weaver's knot*

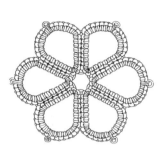

Coats & Clark's Tatting Crochet: 1½in diameter

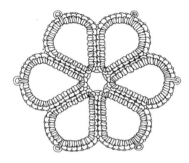

Mercerized Crochet No.30: 1¾in diameter

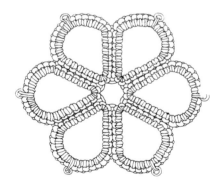

J. & P. Coats Knit Cro-Sheen: 2in diameter

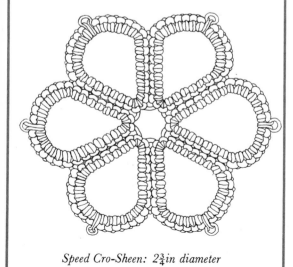

Speed Cro-Sheen: 2¾in diameter

▲ *6-petaled flower magnified to show formation of knots and picots*
▼ *Unusual decoration for towels based on 6-petaled flower, larger rings of double knots and 5 picots, smaller rings of double knots and 3 picots*

Dress-making 29

Tail of a shirt

This chapter continues with blouse conversions from the Creative Pattern Pack given in Volume 22. The fitted shirt is completed and is followed by instructions for making the shirt with tails, pictured on page 578. The shirt with tails is made in a lightweight striped wool. It has flat-fell seams, single cuffs with link buttons, and the body darts are omitted.

The shirt sleeve openings

Before you stitch the sleeve seams, make the openings.
Here are two simple ways to do this.

A. The faced opening. This opening is suitable for both single and link buttoning.
To make a facing, cut a straight piece of fabric from remnants, 2 inches wide and 1 inch longer than the opening indicated on the wrist edge of the sleeve pattern piece. Do not cut the opening yet.
Lay the facing centrally over the opening line on the outside of the sleeve, right sides facing, and baste.
Stitch the facing to the sleeve (figure 1), tapering into a point at the end of the opening.
Cut through the center to within 1 grain of the stitches at the point.
Turn the facing to the inside (figure 2), edge-baste or topstitch close to the edge and press.
Turn in the raw edge of the facing, baste and hem to the sleeve.

B. Opening with wrap extension. This opening is not suitable for link buttoning.
From remnants cut a straight strip of fabric 1½ inches wide and twice the length of the opening.
Cut the sleeve along the opening line (figure 3). Pin and baste the

▼**1.** *Cutting through faced opening*

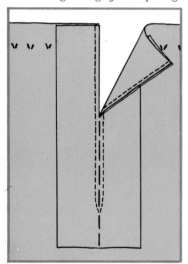

▼**2.** *Basting the faced opening*

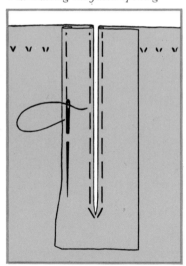

▼**4.** *The facing for the wrap extension stitched to the sleeve opening*

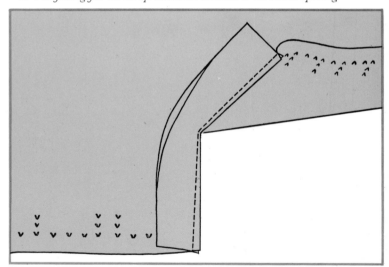

▼ *The fitted shirt*

▼**3.** *Cutting the sleeve-opening*

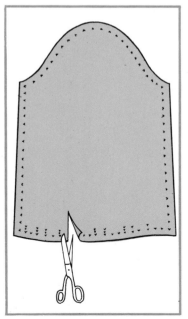

▼**5.** *Pinning the wrap extension strip to the right side of the sleeve*

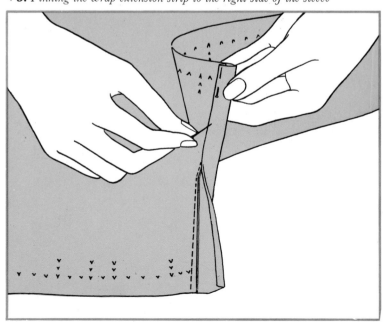

strip of fabric along the opening with the right side of the strip to the wrong side of the sleeve.

Stitch along the opening, taking ¼ inch seam allowance on the facing but tapering toward the point (figure 4).

When you have reached the point, pivot the work on the needle, ease the fold to the back of the needle and stitch along the other side. Press the seam toward the strip.

Fold in the long raw edge of the strip, pin and baste it over the seam on the outside of the sleeve and topstitch (figures 5 and 6). Press the wrap to the inside of the sleeve as shown.

After finishing the opening, stitch sleeve seams with French seam.

Making the cuffs

A. Single cuffs. Fold the interfaced cuffs lengthwise, right sides facing, and stitch each side up to the seam allowance at the top edge. Trim the seam allowance and turn to the right side. Edge-baste and press.

If you want to make single cuffs with link buttoning, stitch the upper edge as far as the two outer balance marks before turning to the right side, as for the double cuff in figure 7. Snip the seam allowance at the balance marks and turn out.

B. Double cuffs. Pin the interfaced and plain sections together, right sides facing.

Stitch around the edges as shown in figure 7. Trim the seam allowance and across the corners. Snip into the seam allowance at the top edge as shown.

Turn the cuffs to the right side, edge-baste and press.

Attaching the cuffs

Gather or pleat the lower edge of the sleeves. The pleats should be folded in the direction of the arrows on the sleeve pattern.

Pin, baste and stitch the cuffs to the right side of the sleeves as shown in figure 8. (Make sure the interfaced section will be uppermost on the finished cuff.)

Turn under the remaining raw edge on each cuff, pin and hand sew it over the seam on the inside (figure 9).

If you wish to topstitch the cuffs ¼ inch from the edge to match the collar stitching, do so now.

Stitching in the sleeves

Stitch the sleeves to the shirt with a French seam.
Press the seam toward the sleeve.

▼ **6.** *The topstitched wrap extension with wrap pressed to the inside*

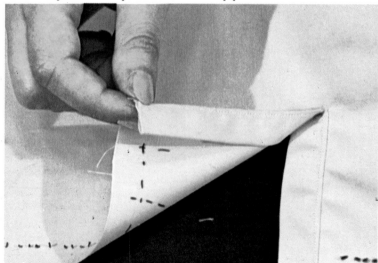

▼ **8.** *Pinning the cuff to the right side of the sleeve*

▼ **7.** *Stitched and trimmed double cuff before turning to the right side*

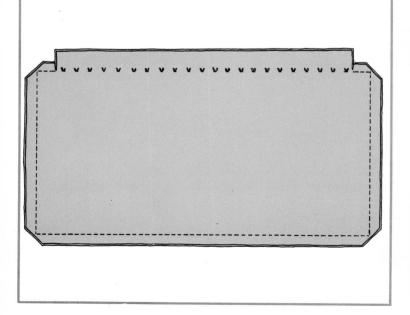

▼ **9.** *Hand sewing the inside cuff edge over the seamline*

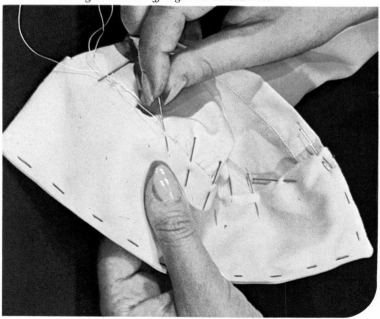

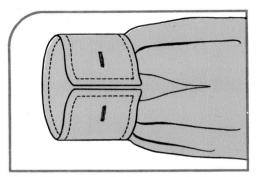

▲ 10. *The single cuff with buttonholes for links*

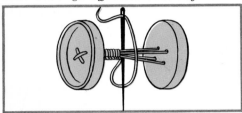

▲ 11. *Making the button link*

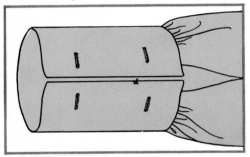

▲ 12. *The double cuff with buttonhole positions*

Buttons and buttonholes

Fitted shirt front. Follow the buttoning for the shirt with tails (figure 13) or, for a more unusual effect, arrange the buttons in groups of three, as shown in the sketch on page 576. Because the shirt is worn tucked in, it is best not to place buttons below the waist as these would bulge underneath a skirt.

Make the buttonholes as shown in Dressmaking chapter 19, page 368, and sew on buttons to correspond.

Single, unlinked cuffs. Make a buttonhole on each cuff on the edge furthest from the sleeve seam (see figure 1 in the previous chapter) and sew on a button to correspond.

Single, linked cuffs (figure 10). Make two buttonholes on each cuff. Make the button links as in figure 11, working the link as for the bar shown in Dressmaking chapter 8, page 156.

Double, linked cuffs (figure 12). These need four buttonholes on each cuff. The thickness of the layers of fabric may cause the under cuff to pucker, so make the buttonholes which go to the top of the cuff $\frac{1}{8}$ inch closer to the edge than those on the underside of the cuff.

Make the button links as in figure 11.

578

Shirt with tails

Fabric requirements and notions

☐ 36in wide fabric: for sizes 32½ and 34in, 3⅛ yards; for size 36in, 3¼ yards; for sizes 38 to 42in, 3⅜ yards.

☐ Interfacing: for all sizes, ⅜ yard. Pre-shrunk lawn for silk fabric and fine poplin for other fabric.

☐ 9 buttons, or 13 for link buttoned cuffs.

☐ Matching thread.

The pattern

Use all the pattern pieces for the fitted shirt.

To make the tails, place the front and back bodice patterns on a sheet of paper at least 3 inches longer than the pattern. Draw around the pattern, then extend the side seams for 3 inches and draw in the new hemline on both pattern pieces, as shown in figure 13.

Draw curves for the tails which taper into the side seams, as shown. To make sure the curve is the same on the back and front, make a paper template, lay it on the extension of the back and front pattern pieces and draw in the new lines.

Then, at the top of the curve on the back, add ½ inch to the side seam and taper into the curve, as shown in figure 14.

▼ 13. *Front pattern with extension and curve*

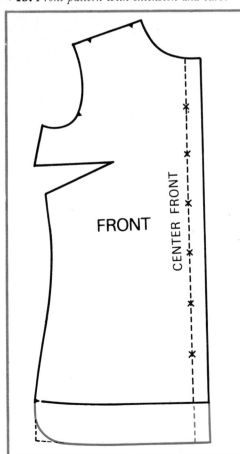

FRONT

CENTER FRONT

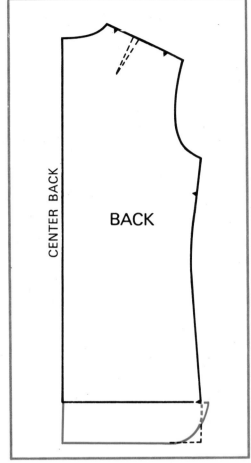

CENTER BACK

BACK

▲ 14. *Back pattern with seam allowance extension*

Make a balance mark on the side seams where the original pattern lengths end; this is the end of the side seam stitching line.

Cut out the new patterns.

Cutting out

Use the cutting instructions and layouts for the fitted shirt in the previous chapter as a guide, making the necessary adjustments to take in the new pattern lengths. The shirt is sewn with flat-fell seams which, like the French seam, require ⅝ inch seam allowances.

Fitting

Follow the fitting instructions for the shirt in the previous chapter, but omit the back and front body darts.

Making the shirt

Follow the instructions for making the fitted shirt, but note the following points.
1. Stitch flat-fell seams instead of French seams. The flat-fell seams are stitched as those in Dressmaking chapter 18, page 356, but this time they are stitched with wrong sides facing and are folded on the outside of the garment, with the folded edge toward the front.

2. Stitch the shoulder and side bust darts only.

3. Position the buttons and buttonholes as shown in figure 13.

4. The hem edge is finished at the side seams as follows.

Hemming the tails. Stitch the side seams to the balance marks, wrong sides facing. Then snip into the front side seam allowance at the bottom of the seams and trim the front seam allowance for flat-fell seaming, as shown in figure 15.

Fold the back seam allowance over the trimmed front seam. Pin and baste.

Pin and baste the hem on the front to the wrong side. Machine stitch and continue the stitching into the folded flat-fell seam edge so that you stitch the hem and flat-fell side seam in one operation, as shown in figure 16.

Pin under the hem on the back. When you reach the point where the side seam and front hem merge, pin the folded edge of the back hem in line with the side seam, as shown in figure 16. Like this, it will lie flat over the top of the front curve and give a neat strong finish. Baste and machine stitch in place.

Stitch across the top of the hem as shown to hold it firmly in place and to strengthen this point.

▼ **15.** *Snipping into the front seam allowance*

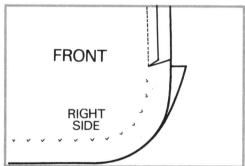

FRONT

RIGHT SIDE

▼ **16.** *The stitched tails at the side seam*

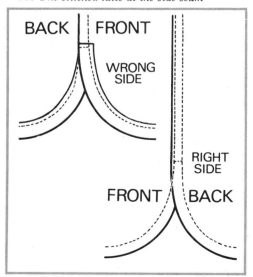

BACK FRONT

WRONG SIDE

RIGHT SIDE

FRONT BACK

Fashion Flair
Rounds about

These simple circular motifs can be interpreted in different embroidery techniques —here are some ideas to try out for fun.

1. *Appliqué brightly colored cotton motifs to a child's denim apron.*
2. *Embroider a wool motif on a sweater, using detached chain and satin stitches.*
3. *Work both motifs in brilliantly colored plastic straw to add a touch of individuality to a beach bag or tote bag.*
4. *Circular motifs make pretty sachets, pincushions or potholders.*
5. *Embroider the sleeves of a crêpe dress using threads matched to the background fabric.*

Pattern Library

Two-tone leaf design

The simplicity of this cross-stitch design is enhanced by using only two tones of one color—in this case, warm orange and its deeper counterpart. The branch and leaf motif is repeated in geometric lines for a crisp, clean look.

The colors in DMC Pearl Cotton are light marigold 402 and burnt orange 400.

This design would look most effective on embroidered tray cloths, napkins, tablecloths and guest towels.

Getting the hang of hems

Knitting Know-how 30

Most knitted garments look neater when finished with a knitted hem or border. The hem will have a better appearance if the rows which are to form the under layer are worked on needles which are one size smaller than those used for the main part of the garment.

Stockinette stitch hem for sweater hem

Cast on the required number of stitches and, beginning with a knit row, work an odd number of rows. Knit the next row instead of purling it to mark the foldline; then, beginning with a knit row, work the same number of rows as were worked initially to complete the hem. When the garment is finished, turn the hem to the wrong side of the work at the foldline and slip stitch in place. This hem is ideal for the bottom of a sweater where a certain amount of elasticity is needed.

Knitted-in hem for coats and jackets

Cast on and work as given for the stockinette stitch hem, working one row less after the foldline to end with a purl row. Before continuing with the garment, pick up the stitches of the cast-on row with an extra needle and hold these stitches behind the stitches already on the left-hand needle. Knit to the end of the next row by working one stitch from the left-hand needle together with one stitch from the extra needle. Beginning with a purl row, continue

▲ *Stockinette stitch hem*   ▼ *Stockinette stitch hem sewed to wrong side*

▲ *Knitted-in hem*   ▼ *Knitted-in hem from right side*

in stockinette stitch. This forms a very firm hemline and is excellent for use on a coat or jacket.

Picot hem for lacy patterns

Cast on an odd number of stitches and, beginning with a knit row, work an even number of rows in stockinette stitch. On the next row, or right side of the work, make a row of picot eyelets by *K2 tog, ytf, and repeat from * to last stitch, K1. Beginning with a purl row, work the same number of rows as were worked initially to complete the hem. When the garment is finished, turn the hem to the wrong side of the work at the picot row and slip stitch in place. This method forms an attractive scalloped edge, suitable for trimming baby garments or for giving a dainty edge to lace patterns.

Reversed stockinette stitch hem for necklines and sleeve edges

When the edging is completed, leave the stitches on the needle instead of binding off and fold the required depth of hem onto the right side of the work, so that the purl side forms the hem. Sew along the edge, taking one stitch from the needle and one stitch from right side. This method is ideal for finishing necklines and for completing skirts which are worked from the waist down. It can also be made by folding the hem to the wrong side to form a plain stockinette stitch edge.

Slip stitch vertical edge for jacket edges

Cast on the required number of stitches, allowing six extra stitches for the border. Work in stockinette stitch across the full width of stitches, but on every knit row slip the sixth stitch in from the required edge of the row knitwise to form a fold line. When the garment is finished, turn the border to the wrong side at the fold line and slip stitch down. This edge is suitable for the front edges of a jacket or a coat which is unbuttoned.

◄ *Picot hem before finishing* ▲ *Picot hem completed*
▼ *Reversed stockinette stitch hem picking up one stitch from the needle*

◄ *Slip stitch border for cardigans*
▼ *Finishing reversed stockinette stitch hem picking up one stitch from right side*

Like mother like daughter

These useful matching cardigans can be made in a wide range of sizes to fit both you and your daughter. The pattern panels are optional and the design may be worked entirely in reversed stockinette stitch. Both cardigans button to the neck for extra warmth and comfort.

Sizes

Directions are for 28in bust or chest.
The figures in brackets [] refer to the 30, 32, 34, 36 and 38in sizes respectively.
Length down center back, 19½[20½:22:23:23½:24]in.
Sleeve seam, 13[14:16:17: 18:18]in.

Gauge
6sts and 8 rows to 1in over stockinette stitch worked on No.5 needles.

Materials
Sports Yarn
4[4:5:6:7:7] 2oz skeins
One pair No.3 needles (or Canadian No.10)
One pair No.5 needles (or Canadian No.8)
Cable needle
Seven buttons

Note
To work the cardigan entirely in reversed stockinette stitch, follow directions exactly as given, omitting the panel patt on fronts and sleeves.

Back

Using No.3 needles, cast on 86[92:98:104:110:116] sts.
Work 1[1:1½:1½:1½:1½]in in

584

K1, P1 rib.
Change to No.5 needles.
Beg with a P row continue in reversed stockinette stitch until work measures 12[12½:13½: 14:14:14]in from beg, ending with a K row.

Shape armholes
Bind off 2sts at beg of next 2 rows.
Dec one st at each end of next and every other row until 24[26:28:30:32:34] sts rem.
Work 1 row.
Bind off.

Left front

Using No.3 needles, cast on 43[46:49:52:55:58] sts.
Work 1[1:1½:1½:1½:1½]in K1, P1 rib.
Change to No.5 needles.
Commence patt:
1st row P25[27:29:32:34:36] sts, K1, P1, K1, P10, K1, P1, K1, P to end.
2nd row K2[3:4:4:5:6] sts, ytf, sl 1, ytb, K1, ytf, sl 1, ytb, K10, ytf, sl 1, ytb, K1, ytf, sl 1, ytb, K to end.
3rd row P25[27:29:32:34:36] sts, K1, P1, sl next st on cable needle and hold at front of work, P next st then K st on cable needle—called C2L—P8, sl next st on cable needle and hold at back of work, K next st then P st on cable needle—called C2R—P1, K1, P to end.
4th row K2[3:4:4:5:6] sts, ytf, sl 1, ytb, K2, ytf, sl 1, ytb, K8, ytf, sl 1, ytb, K2, ytf, sl 1, ytb, K to end.
5th row P25[27:29:32:34:36]

sts, K1, P2, C2L, P6, C2R, P2, K1, P to end.
6th row K2[3:4:4:5:6] sts, sl 1 as before, K3, sl 1, K6, sl 1, K3, sl 1, K to end.
7th row P25[27:29:32:34:36] sts, K1, P3, C2L, P4, C2R, P3, K1, P to end.
8th row K2[3:4:4:5:6] sts, sl 1, (K4, sl 1) 3 times, K to end.
9th row P25[27:29:32:34:36] sts, K1, P4, C2L, P2, C2R, P4, K1, P to end.
10th row K2[3:4:4:5:6] sts, sl 1, K5, sl 1, K2, sl 1, K5, sl 1, K to end.
11th row P25[27:29:32:34:36] sts, K1, P5, C2L, C2R, P5, K1, P to end.
12th row K2[3:4:4:5:6] sts, sl 1, K6, sl 2, K6, sl 1, K to end.
13th row P25[27:29:32:34:36] sts, K1, P6, sl next st onto cable needle and hold at front of work, K next st then K st on cable needle, P6, K1, P to end.
14th row K2[3:4:4:5:6] sts, sl 1, K14, sl 1, K to end.
15th row P25[27:29:32: 34:36] sts, K1, P6, make a bobble on next 2sts by knitting then purling then knitting into each st.
Turn.
Beg with a P row work 4 rows st st on these 6sts.
Now with left-hand needle pass 2nd st over first st, 3rd st over first st, then sl first st back onto left-hand needle. Sl 5th st over 4th st and 6th st over 4th st. Replace first st on right-hand needle, P6, K1, P to end.
16th row K2[3:4:4:5:6] sts sl 1, K14, sl 1, K to end.
These 16 rows form panel patt and are rep throughout.
Continue in patt until work measures same as back to underarm, ending with a WS row.

Shape armhole
Bind off 2sts at beg of next row, patt to end.
Work 1 row.
Dec one st at beg of next and every other row until work measures 17[17½:19:19½:20: 20½]in from beg, ending at center front edge.

Shape neck
Bind off 6sts at beg of next row and dec one st at neck edge on the next 5[6:7:8:9: 10] rows; *at the same time* continue to dec at armhole edge as before until 2sts rem. K2 tog. Fasten off.

Right front

Work as given for left front, reversing all shaping and noting that first patt row will read as follows:
1st row P2[3:4:4:5:6] sts, K1, P1, K1, P10, K1, P1, K1, P to end.

Sleeves

Using No.3 needles, cast on 42[44:46:48:50:52] sts.
Work 2[2:2½:2½:2½:2½]in K1, P1 rib.
Change to No.5 needles.
Commence patt:
1st row P13[14:15:16:17: 18] sts, K1, P1, K1, P10, K1, P1, K1, P to end.
2nd row K13[14:15:16:17: 18] sts, sl 1, K1, sl 1, K10, sl 1, K1, sl 1, K to end.
These 2 rows form patt.
Continue in patt as given for left front, keeping center 16 sts in patt and inc one st at each end of 5th and every following 6th row until there are 66[70:74:80:84:88] sts.
Continue without shaping until sleeve measures 13 [14:16:17:18:18]in from beg, ending with a WS row.

Shape cap
Bind off 2sts at beg of next 2 rows.
Dec one st at each end of next and every other row until 4[4:4:6:6:6] sts rem. Work 1 row.
Bind off.

Borders

Using No.3 needles, cast on 10sts.
Work in K1, P1 rib.
Work ¾[1¼:1¼:½:1¼:½]in.
Next row (buttonhole row) Rib 3, bind off 3sts, rib to end.
Next row Rib 3, cast on 3 sts, rib to end.
Make 5 more buttonholes in

this way at intervals of 2¾[2¾:3:3¼:3¼:3½]in, measured from the center of the previous buttonhole. Continue until border measures 17[17½:19:19½:20:20½] in from beg. Bind off in rib.

Work other border in same way, omitting buttonholes.

Finishing

Press lightly.
Join raglan, side and sleeve seams using backstitch and oversewing welts and cuffs.
Attach borders to center front edges from RS (P side).

Neckband

Using No.3 needles, with RS facing, pick up and K85 [93:97:107:115:119] sts evenly around neck.
Work 7[7:8:8:8:8] rows K1, P1 rib making buttonhole as before on 4th and 5th rows.
Bind off in rib.
Sew on buttons.

Captivating crochet

Make this delightful, triangular crocheted headscarf to guard against playful breezes. It is worked in a simple chainmail stitch and buttons neatly under the chin so that it cannot slip off.

▲ *Front view and button fastening*
▼ *Back view showing edging*

Size
To fit an average head

Materials
Sports Yarn
One 2oz ball
One No.C (2.50 mm)
crochet hook
1 button

Headscarf

Ch6. Join into a loop by working 1sc into the first ch worked. Turn and work first row into top of this loop.
1st row Ch6, 1sc into first of 6ch, ch5, 1sc into 3rd ch of loop. Turn.
2nd row Ch6, 1sc into first of 6ch, (ch5, 1sc into 3rd ch of next loop) twice. Turn.
3rd row Ch6, 1sc into first of 6ch, (ch5, 1sc into 3rd ch of next loop) 3 times. Turn.
4th, 5th, 6th, 7th and 8th rows are worked as for 3rd row, but inc number of times sts in parentheses are worked by one rep more each row.
9th row Ch5, 1sc into 3rd ch of first 5ch loop, (ch5, 1sc into 3rd ch of next loop) 10 times. Turn.
10th row As 9th.
11th row Ch6, 1sc into first of 6ch, (ch5, 1sc into 3rd ch of next loop) 11 times. Turn. Continue in this way, inc one loop on each of 8 rows, then working 2 rows without inc. Rep until 36 rows have been worked.

Edging
Do not turn at end of last row.
1st row Work 84sc evenly along side to back point (formed by first loop), 84sc along other side to front edge, work 3sc into each loop along this front edge. Join to first sc with ss.
2nd row Work 1sc into each sc working 2sc into each of 3 sc at each corner. Join to first sc with ss.
3rd row *Ch7, 1sc into next sc, rep from * to end of 2nd side only, skipping the front edge. Finish off.

Finishing
Do not press.
Sew button to left-hand front corner using first loop at right-hand front corner as a buttonhole.

Marigolds, sweet marigolds

Embroidery

30

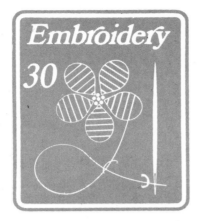

These golden flowers of summer, embroidered in flaming shades of orange on a crisp cloth, bring the warm glow of sunny days to your table. This sunlit effect is achieved by the different treatment of the petals of each flower.

Ways with the motifs

These charming flower motifs can be used in a variety of ways. For instance, they can be arranged in the center of a tablecloth or scattered all over the surface. Arrange the individual motifs in two parallel lines down the center of a long cloth, or in a cluster in the middle and bordering the edge of a circular cloth.

For a gay peasant effect, embroider the flowers on dark blue linen or on the same bright green as the flower hearts.

▼ *The design outline to trace and one idea for placing the motifs*

Fabric

Make a tablecloth to the shape and size you want .(following the instructions in Embroidery chapter 21, page 414) or buy a ready-made cloth in a plain, smooth-textured fabric such as cotton or linen or one of the synthetic no-iron fabrics.

Yarns and stitches

The design illustrated is worked in 6-strand embroidery floss in orange, light orange and bright green. The sunlit effect of the posies is achieved by the treatment of the petals. The deeper-colored flowers are worked in satin stitch using three strands, the lighter flowers in long and short stitch using three strands, and the white flowers are outlined in outline stitch using two strands.

Planning the design

Plan your design by tracing several motifs on paper, and then cut them out. Lay the tablecloth flat and arrange the cut-out motifs until they make a pleasing effect. Keep the motifs pinned to the cloth until you are ready to transfer the design to the cloth (see Embroidery chapter 4, page 68) ready for embroidering.

It is a mistake to overcrowd a design on a tablecloth. If you scatter the motifs over the cloth, do not work embroidery where it will be covered by a plate or may perhaps create an uneven surface for glasses. An interesting effect can be created by using the flower motifs for appliqué. Work the flowers on separate pieces of fabric, cut them out and appliqué them to the tablecloth, overcasting the edges, using thread which matches the embroidery.

▼ *Complement your embroidery with a centerpiece of matching flowers as displayed on this European table setting*

Bobbin Lace 3

Background to bobbin lace

Before progressing to decorative lace patterns, it is good preparation to try these three plain mesh stitches which are backgrounds for linking motifs. You will gradually learn how to cope with more bobbins and your first lace pattern will be well within your capabilities. Trace the chart onto cardboard and extend the pattern as far as necessary.

Mesh stitch with one twist

Copy the chart as illustrated.
Place 2 pairs of bobbins on each of points **a, b, c, d, e,** of the chart. Turn and cross the 2nd and 3rd pairs of bobbins and fix with a pin at point No.**1**, then make another half stitch with the same bobbins.
Turn and cross the 1st and 2nd pairs, fix a pin at point No.**2**; make a half stitch.
Turn and cross the 4th and 5th pairs, fix a pin at point No.**3**; make a half stitch.
Turn and cross the 3rd and 4th pairs, fix a pin at point No.**4**; make a half stitch.
Turn and cross the 2nd and 3rd pairs, fix a pin at point No.**5**; make a half stitch.
Turn and cross the 1st and 2nd pairs, fix a pin at point No.**6**; make a half stitch.
Begin again from the 6th and 7th pairs, turning and crossing them, fix a pin at point No.**7**; make a half stitch.
Continue the work until you reach point No.**12**.
Begin again, turning and crossing the 8th and 9th pairs, fix a pin at point No.**13**; make a half stitch.
Continue in the same way, following the rows of consecutive numbers on the diagram.
Work the lace diagonally until you reach the length you require. To finish the work and even it off, work some incomplete diagonals, making a rectangle.

Mesh stitch with two twists

This stitch is also worked diagonally, using the same chart.
Place two pairs of bobbins on each of points **a, b, c, d, e.**
Turn the 2nd and 3rd pairs twice and cross them, fix a pin at point No.**1**; with the same bobbins make a half stitch.
Turn the 1st and 2nd pairs twice and cross them, fix a pin at point No.**2**; make a half stitch.
Turn the 4th and 5th pairs twice and cross them, fix a pin at point No.**3**; make a half stitch.
Turn the 3rd and 4th pairs twice and cross them, fix a pin at point No.**4**; make a half stitch.
Turn the 2nd and 3rd pairs twice and cross them, fix a pin at point

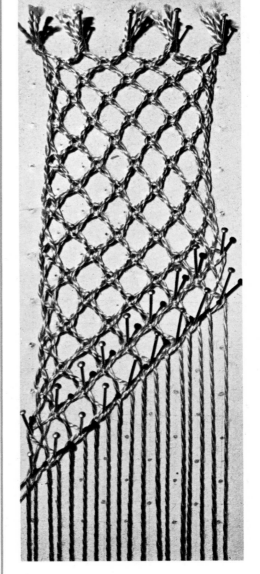

The green mesh background pictured on the left is worked with one twist. The yellow mesh, pictured right, is worked with two twists. Both are worked from the same pattern, starting with two pairs of bobbins at each point, giving a total of twenty bobbins.

No.**5**; make a half stitch.
Turn the 1st and 2nd pairs twice and cross them, fix a pin at point No.**6**; make a half stitch.
Turn the 6th and 7th pairs twice and cross them, fix a pin at point No.**7**; make a half stitch.
Continue like this until the pin is fixed at point No.**12**.
Begin again from point No.**13** and continue diagonally to point No.**20**. Continue the work, following the diagonal number order of the chart. Finish off the lace by working some incomplete rows to even it off.

Plain open-work stitch

Copy the chart as illustrated.
Fix 2 pairs of bobbins on each of points **a, b, c, d, e, f.**
Turn and cross the 1st and 2nd pairs of bobbins, the 3rd and 4th pairs, the 2nd and 3rd pairs, fix a pin at point No.**1**; make a half stitch with the last set of bobbins.
Turn and cross the 1st and 2nd pairs, fix a pin at point No.**2**; make a half stitch.

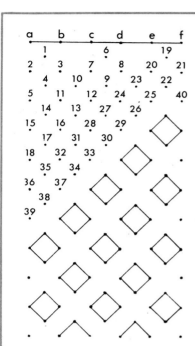

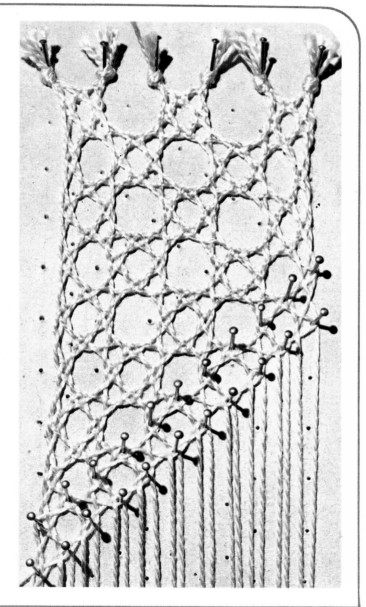

Plain open-work stitch, pictured right, is a background stitch which is pretty enough to use on its own. For example, make an inset for table linen or a dress. Worked from six points there is a total of twenty-four bobbins. At first, it is difficult to keep so many bobbins in the correct order but gradually you will find it easier to manage.

Turn and cross the 3rd and 4th pairs, fix a pin at point No.**3**; make a half stitch.

Turn and cross the 2nd and 3rd pairs, fix a pin at point No.**4**; make a half stitch.

Turn and cross the 1st and 2nd pairs, fix a pin at point No.**5**; make a half stitch.

Turn and cross * the 3rd and 4th pairs, the 5th and 6th pairs, the 7th and 8th pairs, the 6th and 7th pairs, fix a pin at point No.**6**; make a half stitch.

Turn and cross the 5th and 6th pairs, fix a pin at point No.**7**; make a half stitch.

Turn and cross the 7th and 8th pairs, fix a pin at point No.**8**; make a half stitch.

Turn and cross the 6th and 7th pairs, fix a pin at point No.**9**; make a half stitch.

Turn and cross the 5th and 6th pairs, the 4th and 5th pairs, fix a pin at point No.**10**; make a half stitch.

Turn and cross the 3rd and 4th pairs, fix a pin at point No.**11**; make a half stitch.

Turn and cross the 5th and 6th pairs, fix a pin at point No.**12**; make a half stitch.

Turn and cross the 4th and 5th pairs, fix a pin at point No.**13**; make a half stitch.

Turn and cross the 3rd and 4th, the 2nd and 3rd pairs, fix a pin at point No.**14**; make a half stitch.

Turn and cross the 1st and 2nd pairs, fix a pin at point No.**15**; make a half stitch.

Turn and cross the 3rd and 4th pairs, fix a pin at point No.**16**; make a half stitch.

Turn and cross the 2nd and 3rd pairs, fix a pin at point No.**17**; make a half stitch.

Turn and cross the 1st and 2nd pairs, fix a pin at point No.**18**; make a half stitch.

Turn and cross the pairs of bobbins as from *.

Continue up to the 7th and 8th pairs, then go on with the other pairs of bobbins. Continue, following the numerical order of the chart.

Finishing

There is no specific way of finishing lace. You can tie the ends in knots similar to the ones at the beginning, and then either darn in the threads or roll a hem.

Furnishing Fashion Flair

Toytown train

This happy little train, with an engine, two cars, and a caboose, makes a charming design to brighten a child's world. What little boy wouldn't jump for joy to have these trains running around his bed? And it would be an ideal border for curtains, embroidered in brilliant colors using outline stitches. For the playroom, create a magnificent appliquéd picture and decorated wastebasket to match. Cut the design out of contact paper and stick it to the top of the toy chest. Make a gay and practical placemat for your little Casey Jones in brightly embroidered linen accompanied by a cup decorated with the motif. The possibilities are endless once you get started on this easy and versatile design.

Needles, threads and stitches

Dress-
making
30

Sew special

With the wide and ever increasing range of fabrics on the market, both in natural and man-made fibers, it is important to realize that now there is the right sewing thread for every type of fabric. Successful dressmaking depends on using the right thread because if both thread and fabric share the same characteristics, they can be laundered together, ironed at the same temperatures and will also shrink and stretch together.

Types of thread
The natural threads are silk and cotton. Cotton thread is mercerized or unmercerized. Mercerized cotton is specially treated to give it luster and greater strength. Silk thread is a multi-purpose thread and combines strength with elasticity.
Of synthetic threads, the most commonly used are those made from polyester fiber.

Thicknesses
Threads, whether natural or synthetic, are produced in various thicknesses; the higher the number the finer the thread. The most commonly used thickness is 50, but for finer fabrics 60 can be used. When machine stitching, it is important to remember that whatever you use on the spool you should also use on the bobbin.

Sewing synthetics
When sewing man-made fiber fabrics, and mixtures of natural and man-made fibers, a synthetic thread should be used.
Synthetic thread is usually stronger than natural thread and an interesting feature is its stretchability, which is particularly important when sewing fabrics with stretch, such as synthetic knits. With these fabrics a great deal of stress is put upon the seams during movement and activity, so if the thread can stretch with the fabric it minimizes the chance of broken stitching.
Cotton-wrapped polyester thread is also suitable for sewing fine leather which has a good deal of stretch in it.

Sewing cotton and linen
For these fabrics a mercerized cotton thread is used for most purposes. If you sew cotton or linen fabric with a synthetic thread, it will not be able to withstand the heat required for pressing and will melt.
Unmercerized cotton is used for basting; not having the polished surface of mercerized thread it does not slip out as easily.

Sewing wool and silk
Wool can be sewn with silk thread or a mercerized cotton. Always sew pure silk with a fine, lustrous pure silk thread.

Fabric	Fiber	Thread	Needle sizes Hand-sewing	Machine-stitching	Stitches per inch
Fine such as lawn, georgette, voile, chiffon, organdy, net, lace	synthetic and mixtures	synthetic extra fine	9–10	9 to 11	12 to 15
	cotton and linen	mercerized 50	9	9 to 11	12 to 16
	wool	mercerized 50 or silk	9	9 to 11	12 to 16
	silk	silk	9	9 to 11	12 to 14
Lightweight such as poplin, gingham, silk, cotton	synthetic and mixtures	synthetic	8–9	11 to 14	12 to 15
	cotton and linen	mercerized 50	8–9	11 to 14	12 to 15
	wool	mercerized 50 or silk	8–9	11 to 14	12 to 15
	silk	silk	8–9	11 to 14	12 to 15
Medium-weight such as gabardine, brocade, tweed, water-proofed fabrics	synthetic and mixtures	synthetic	8–9	11 to 14	10 to 12
	cotton	mercerized 50	7–8	11 to 14	12 to 15
	linen	mercerized 40	7–8	11 to 14	12 to 14
	wool	mercerized 50 or silk	7–8	11 to 14	12 to 14
	silk	silk	7–8	11 to 14	12 to 14
Heavy-weight such as coatings, canvas, heavy home furnishing fabrics	synthetic and mixtures	synthetic	6	16 to 18	10 to 12
	cotton	mercerized 40	7–8	14 to 16	10 to 12
	linen	mercerized 40	6–7	14 to 18	10 to 12
	wool	mercerized 40 or silk	7–8	14 to 16	10 to 12
	silk	silk	7–8	14 to 16	10 to 12
Some special fabrics					
velvet	synthetic and mixtures	synthetic	8–9	11 to 14	10 to 12
	cotton	mercerized 50	7–8	11 to 14	10 to 12
	silk	silk	7–8	11 to 14	10 to 12
fine leather and vinyl		synthetic		14 to 18	8 to 10

Threads for decorative stitching

For decorative stitching, such as saddle stitching, topstitching, channel seaming and some hand-worked buttonholes, buttonhole twist is used. This is a special, thick silk used to emphasize stitching and is not to be confused with button thread, which is an extra strong waxed thread used to sew buttons on men's clothing, overalls or shoes.

Having stated the importance of using the same thread on both the bobbin and the spool, buttonhole twist is an exception. It is used either on the bobbin or on the spool. Just remember four things about buttonhole twist.

1. If used on the spool, slacken the spool tension.
2. If used on the bobbin, slacken the bobbin tension.
3. If used on the bobbin, stitch from the wrong side of the garment to achieve the desired effect on the right side of the work.
4. A thicker needle and larger stitch length is required.

In most cases, a 40 mercerized cotton is a suitable companion thread to buttonhole twist but it is best to experiment first with your own machine to find the right combination.

Threads for sewing home furnishing and upholstery fabrics

Here a very strong durable thread is needed because it has to stand up to a great deal of stress and hard wear. A polyester and cotton fiber mixture is ideal for this work. In this thread the cotton is wrapped around the polyester fiber, otherwise the very strong polyester strands used would cut the fibers of the fabric. In appearance it is similar to button thread.

This thread is also used on canvas, thick leather and suede.

Other threads

There are other threads on the market, such as embroidery threads, invisible thread, and so on, but this chapter concentrates on those which are most used in dressmaking.

A word on color

Always choose a thread one or two shades darker than the fabric as this will work in lighter, becoming the same color as the fabric.

Needles

It is important to use the correct size needle for the particular thread and fabric. As a general rule, the lighter the fabric, the finer the needle should be. The chart here shows you at a glance the needle and thread sizes for various weights and types of fabric. There are also different types of needles. A ball point needle is specially made for knitted fabrics so that the needle will not cut the fibers of the fabric and cause it to run. There are spear point needles specially made for leather and suede.

Keep a range of hand-sewing and machine needles handy in various sizes and always remember to keep them sharp and straight —don't wait for your needle to break before changing it.

Tension and stitch length

Many sewing faults are traced back to old machine needles and the use of the wrong thread and tension. Therefore, once you have chosen the fabric, the appropriate thread and needles, and before you start stitching on the garment, test on a double scrap of the same fabric to find the correct tension. Also, be sure to test the stitch length to see if it has the right appearance, counting the stitches per inch as given in the chart. If you see the fabric puckering it may mean there are too many stitches to the inch, in which case you will need to make the stitches larger. Test until you are satisfied—it is well worthwhile.

Vogue Couturier Pattern reflects the result of perfect seaming ▶

Fling yourself into kilt-making

The most famous of all pleated skirts is, of course, the Scottish kilt. An authentic kilt is very full and heavy and made from yards of fabric, but there are many ways this can be pared down and still resemble the original.

This chapter gives you a simple method for working out the pleating and calculating yardage for any size, and for skirt lengths up to 23 inches. But if you like the elegant look of the full length version shown here, you can make it from a commercial pattern and use Creative Hands pleating know-how to help you achieve perfect results.

Choosing your fabric

Although kilts are associated with Scottish tartans, they can be made in other fabrics, including plain cloths, provided that the fabric pleats well (see the suggestions for the child's pleated skirt and the knife-pleated skirt in Dressmaking 13, p. 256 & 15, p. 294). The authentic fabric for kilts is a fine wool and because of the amount of fabric used it is best not to choose anything too heavy or bulky.

If you are choosing a man-made or mixture cloth for the adult kilt, make sure that it will respond to being pressed and molded as a natural fiber does. This is important if you want to make the best of the fitted lines on this pleated garment.

Points on pleating

The kilt is fully pleated, which means the length of the pleat fold is the same as the pleat distance (see Dressmaking chapter 13).

Since it is a bulky garment to make and handle, it is a good idea to practice first on a child's kilt, then you can make one for yourself from the same working sequence.

Working out the pleating

This requires a little mathematics, but it is simple if you follow the step-by-step chart shown here. First, take note of the following points:

1. The kilt is fitted, so calculate the amount of fabric needed by the hip measurement, which is the largest part of the body it has to cover.

2. The width of the plain front panel is in proportion to the hip measurement and takes up about one quarter of the circumference. This can be varied, however, to suit your own taste. When dividing measurements for the panel, calculate to the nearest inch —it is so much easier.

3. Allow plenty of ease when you take the hip measurement, as the thickness of the layers of fabric will take it up. The chart shows you how much ease to add.

4. The calculations for the adult and the child's kilt are the same and are based on a 54 inch wide fabric.

Full length for glamour. A handsome kilt made in Menzies tartan

What to do	For example	For your own use
1. Take the hip measurement and add 3in ease.	Making a kilt for a 30in hip and 25in waist, with 8in panel and 1in pleats. 30in+3in=33in	....in+3in=....in
2. Deduct the width of the panel. This gives you the area to be pleated and also the number of pleats.	33in—8in=25in (25 pleats)	....in—....in=....in (....pleats)
3. Multiply by three. This gives you the fabric needed for pleating.	25in×3in=75in	....in×3in=....in
4. Add twice the panel width (the kilt has a double wrap-over).	(8in×2=16in) 75in+16in=91in	(....in×2=....in) ....in+....in=....in
5. Add the seam allowance ($\frac{1}{2}$in) for each pleated section to be joined together.	91in+1in=92in	....in+....in=....in
6. To finish the upper front panel add 5in.	92in+5in=97in	....in+5in=....in
7. To finish the under front panel add 1in.	97in+1in=98in =the total width of the skirt.	....in+1in=....in

How much fabric to buy

The example in the chart gives a skirt width of 98 inches, which easily fits across two widths of 54 inch fabric, or twice the skirt length. But if the total width of the skirt exceeds 105 inches, an extra skirt length is needed for the additional pleats. There will, of course, be an extra seam which must be allowed for.

For the total yardage add $3\frac{1}{2}$ inches on each skirt length for the waist seam and hem allowance, and $2\frac{1}{2}$-3 inches for the waistband. If you are buying a check or tartan, make sure that the pattern can be matched across all sections and that you buy enough fabric to enable you to do this.

As explained, all the instructions for working out the fabric in this chapter are based on a 54 inch width. It is possible, however, to use narrower fabric, but there will be more seams in the pleating.

Royal Stewart tartan gives this girl's kilt an authentic Scottish air ▶

Take care 4

Ironing versus pressing

Not many people realize that ironing and pressing are two totally separate, completely different techniques. Ironing is the method best suited to getting wrinkles and creases out of linen, cotton, and other firmly woven, thin fabrics. It consists of a to-and-fro stroking and smoothing action. Pressing, on the other hand, is used on fabrics that stretch, such as double-knit, jersey, and wool knits. In pressing, the iron is placed on the material, which should be covered with a pressing cloth, and then lifted again. If the instructions say press they mean just that; the ironing motion can distort, stretch or flatten the fabric.

Ironing temperatures

Whatever the fabric it is important that ironing be continued until the fabric is dry. Garments left slightly damp will wrinkle and, if left in a confined space, may develop mold spots. The chart on page 600 gives electric iron settings for ironing different fabrics.

Pressing procedure

Pressing is done on the wrong side of the material wherever possible except, of course, when pressing lined garments. Delicate fabrics and garments which do not require steam pressing should be pressed with a piece of dry muslin between the iron and the garment. If steam is required, for reviving a fabric or restoring shape to a garment, a damp cloth or a steam iron can be used. A piece of cotton, flannel or linen can be used as a pressing cloth.

Heavy materials are best pressed on a thickly padded ironing board with a piece of flannel between the garment and the damp cloth. This padding helps to avoid a flattened 'ironed' look.

Soak the pressing cloth in a bowl of water placed conveniently near the ironing board, wring it out thoroughly and lay it over the part of the garment to be pressed. Use a moderately hot iron and press firmly, lifting the iron with each movement. If a skirt has seated, or trousers have bagged at the knees, the pressing cloth should be wet. Place the wet cloth on the area to be shrunk and press. Bang the steam which rises back into the garment with the back of a clothes brush and be careful not to stretch the cloth. Different fabrics require different degrees of pressure and dampness. A fair guide is that the lighter the fabric, the lighter the touch and the drier the cloth.

Although many shirts and trousers are no-iron today, the dressmaker who wants a really professional look to her garments will want to know how to press and iron her products.

Cleaning the iron sole plate

The sole plate of an electric iron can mark garments if it is not kept scrupulously clean. If stains and marks develop from ironing starched items, rub the sole plate with a damp cloth while the iron is still warm. If marks are long-standing, remove them by rubbing with lemon juice.

Ironing a shirt

Set the iron to the correct reading for the shirt fabric—hot, for cotton or linen. The shirt should be slightly and evenly damp. Turn the garment inside out and iron the yoke, pleat heading, seams and hems until they are dry. Turn the shirt to the right side and iron the collar, both inside and outside, and then the cuffs, stretching the material taut and ironing until the fabric is quite dry. Next, iron the sleeves, using a sleeve board if available, or fold the sleeve along the underarm seam and iron to within ¼ inch of the outer fold. Then refold and iron the unironed strip, taking care not to make a sharp crease along the sleeve. Do both sleeves in the same way, setting the pleat in the cuff edge.

Iron first the back and then the front of the shirt, working the point of the iron around the buttons and taking care with the shoulders. Fasten the buttons and iron the front again, and, if there is a pocket, press it flat.

Turn the shirt over and lay it front downward. Fold the fronts back on the shirt so that the sleeves lie flat on the shirt back (see diagram). You will find that a piece of cardboard cut to measure 14 inches long and 7 inches wide will be of help in keeping the two sides equally folded. Slip the cardboard out. Fold the shirt tail up about one third of the length of the shirt, and then fold again.

Pressing a pair of trousers

The waist and upper part of trousers are pressed first. Open the waistband and front fastening and slip the trousers onto the end of the ironing board. Begin by pressing the right fly front and then move the garment around and press the area of the right pocket. Move the garment around on the board again and press the back waist seam, and then on again and press the left pocket and the left fly front. Use the left hand to flatten pocket linings as you press. Lift the trousers from the ironing board and, holding them by the waist, bring both waist pleats together. With the right hand, grasp the trouser leg bottoms and reverse the trousers so that the waist hangs down, the leg creases in line with the waist pleats. Lay the trousers on the ironing board with the left leg underneath. Turn the right trouser leg back so that the inner seam of the left leg and the crotch is exposed. Press, and, holding the leg bottom edges even, stretch the leg to reshape the knee. Press the front and back creases firmly. Bring the right trouser leg back over the pressed leg and turn the trousers over. Turn the pressed left leg back carefully and press the right in the same way as the left.

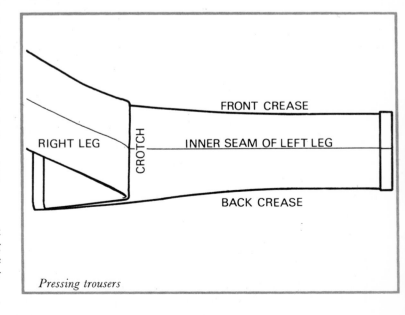

Pressing trousers

▲ *Iron the yoke on the inside, then smooth seams on the outside*
▼ *Iron the collar on both the inside and the outside*

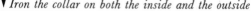

▼ *Stretch the material as the cuffs are ironed*

▼ *Be careful not to make a crease on the sleeve*

▼ *Iron the back of the shirt first, then the front*

▲ *Fasten the buttons and iron the front again*

▼ *Fold the front so that the sleeves lie flat*

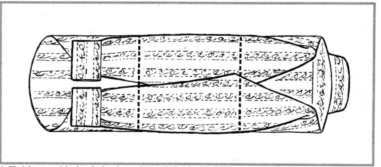

▲ *Fold one third of the length and fold again*

▼ *A perfectly ironed shirt*

Ironing & pressing guide

Test the fabric for yourself, as so much depends on individual fabrics

Fabric	Method of pressing and ironing
Iron setting: Cool	
Acrilan, Orlon, Courtelle, brushed nylon, synthetic organza.	Dry press, muslin for protection if needed. Light pressure on jersey fabrics.
Iron setting: Warm	
Acetate rayon: (satin, taffeta, lining fabrics, brocade, crêpe, ottoman, metallic fabric, surah, chiffon). Plain nylon, nylon jersey, net lace. Tricelon (ninon, voile, georgette). Synthetics: (lawn, surah, chiffon, net, jersey, Dacron). Stretch fabrics.	Dry press, protect right side with dry muslin. Very light pressure on crêpe, jersey, or fabrics with raised surface.
Iron setting: Medium	
Viscose rayon (linen-look, brushed gabardine, spun rayon). Silk (shantung, brocade, dupioni, Japanese, taffeta, crêpe de chine, satin, peau de soie, cloqué, jersey, moiré, matelassé). Heavy and medium suit weight silk (tussore), raw silk. Wool (jersey, dress weight, bouclé, crêpe, georgette, velour, textured wool). Dacron/wool. Acrilan/wool. Synthetic tweed, synthetic/wool.	Often requires damp muslin. Firm pressure. Light pressure, press on wrong side, or if a little right side pressing is essential, protect with dry muslin. Damp muslin, firm pressure. Firm pressure and damp muslin on plain wool. Block if necessary. Light pressure, damp muslin on jersey. Very light pressure, damp muslin with dry one beneath, for bouclé, georgette, crêpe. Firm pressure, damp muslin, block if needed. Light pressure, damp muslin. If very soft use dry muslin and damp one on top.
Iron setting: Hot	
Worsteds (suiting, gabardine, barathea, hopsack, twill). Woolens (flannel, reversible cloth, tweed, coatings, camel, mohair). Cotton (poplin, sailcloth, gingham, twill, piqué, brushed cotton). Cotton (corduroy, velveteen, suede cloth). Linen (dress and suit weight linen, twill, jacquard).	Damp sheeting, pressing block. Light pressure and slightly damp muslin for mohair. Firm pressure, dry press. Thick types may need use of damp muslin, if so, dry off with iron on wrong side only. Press lightly on wrong side, slightly damp muslin. Avoid finger marks while warm. Brush up right side with clothes brush. Press only short-pile velveteens like this. Longer pile, more luxurious ones need pressing over a needle board, or steaming. Firm pressure, damp muslin, may need to be dried off, on wrong side only, with iron. Will shine if pressed on right side with bare iron; iron on wrong side or protect with muslin.

Care of problem fabrics

Angora
Pure angora is a fluffy rabbit wool, but angora and nylon are frequently mixed. Both pure angora and the blend are treated in the same way.
Angora requires no ironing.

Cashmere
Cashmere is woven from the soft hair combed from the Kashmir goat.
Iron on the wrong side under a damp cloth to restore elasticity.

Corduroy
Minimum ironing is required. Work on the wrong side of the fabric with the garment resting on layers of toweling.

Crêpe and crêpe de chine
Real silk crêpe and crêpe de chine require the same careful handling as silk.
Iron garments on the wrong side with a warm iron, while the fabric is slightly damp.

Flock-printed fabrics
If smoothing with an iron is necessary, iron on the wrong side, using a warm iron.

Georgette
Georgettes made of man-made fibers are easy to care for, but fabrics made from pure silk or wool are more difficult.
When almost dry, iron carefully on the wrong side, using as much heat as the fabric will allow and considerable pressure. The garment must be ironed until it is dry, or it may shrink while it is hanging in the closet waiting to be worn.

Metallic thread fabrics
Iron garments carefully with warm iron, whatever the fabric. A hot iron may melt the metallic threads.

Satin
Silk satin should be ironed like silk. Acetate satin should be ironed while it is slightly damp. If acetate satin becomes overdry it should be rolled in a damp towel for a short time. Do not sprinkle with water or use a steam iron, as this fabric spots very easily.

Silk
Iron garments on the wrong side with a warm iron, while the fabric is slightly damp.

Taffeta
While the fabric is slightly damp, iron with a warm iron on the wrong side. If the material becomes too dry, do not sprinkle with water, but wrap the garment in a wet towel for 10 minutes, then iron.

Velvet
If the pile needs reviving, it is safer to steam velvet rather than press it.
To steam velvet, stand a hot iron on end, cover it with a damp cloth and hold the wrong side of the velvet against it. Be careful not to handle the velvet too much while it is damp, or it may mark.
If marks persist, brush with a dense clothes brush in the direction of the pile.

Velveteen
Velveteen is generally made from cotton, but sometimes rayon. It should not need ironing, but if a finishing is required; iron very lightly on the wrong side while the fabric is slightly damp.

Wool
Ironing is usually unnecessary with wool garments, but if a particular garment calls for a flat smooth finish, press lightly on the wrong side, using a warm iron.

Pattern Library

Plum and orange motif
This simple motif is embroidered in chain, outline and satin stitches. Simple enough for a child to work, it would make a gay splash of color on an apron or potholder. The colors used here are in D.M.C. Matte Embroidery cotton—Nasturtium, 2351; Tangerine, 2742; Jade, 2912 and White.

The simple shapes of this design would easily adapt to appliqué work. Trace the shapes and transfer them onto scraps of bright, textured fabric for children's clothes.

Sasha and Gregor dolled up

Sasha and Gregor look adorable in their matching waistcoats, designed to coordinate with the pullover and pants in Knitting Know-how 25, page 482. These little patterns give you a chance to practice cable stitch on the waistcoat and increasing and decreasing on the cap.

You will need
3-ply fingering yarn
3 ounces
Small quantity of contrast for pompon
One pair No.3 needles (or Canadian No.10)
One cable needle
Small stitch holder

Gauge
7 sts and 9 rows to 1in over stockinette stitch worked on No.3 needles.

Waistcoat right front

Using No.3 needles, cast on 21 sts.
K 4 rows.
Continue in patt.
1st row Sl 1, K2, P8, K4, P6.
2nd row K6, P4, K11.
Rep 1st and 2nd rows once more.
5th row Sl 1, K2, P8, sl next 2 sts onto cable needle and hold at front of work, K2 from left-hand needle, K2 from cable needle—called C4F—P6.
6th row As 2nd.
Rep 1st-6th rows 6 times more.

Shape armhole and front edge
Next row Sl 1, K2, P2 tog,

Knitting Know-how 31

---

patt to last 2 sts, P2 tog.
Next row K2 tog, patt to end.
Next row Sl 1, K2, patt to last 2 sts, P2 tog.
Next row K2 tog, patt to end.
Keeping cable patt correct, P2 tog inside 3 edge sts on next and every 4th row until 11 sts rem. Work 3 rows without shaping. Leave sts on holder.

Left front

Using No.3 needles, cast on 21 sts.
K 4 rows.
Continue in patt.
1st row P6, K4, P8, K3.
2nd row Sl 1, K10, P4, K6.
Rep 1st and 2nd rows once more.
5th row P6, C4F, P8, K3.
6th row As 2nd.
Rep 1st-6th rows 6 times more.

Shape armhole
Next row P2 tog, patt to last 5 sts, P2 tog tbl, K3.
Next row Sl 1, patt to last 2 sts, K2 tog.
Next row P2 tog, patt to last 3 sts, K3.
Next row Sl 1, patt to last 2 sts, K2 tog.
Keeping cable patt correct, P2 tog tbl inside 3 edge sts on next and every 4th row until 11 sts rem. Work 3 rows without shaping.

Work back
1st row Work across left front sts thus—P2, K4, P2, K3, turn, cast on 12 sts, turn and continue across sts for right front thus—K3, P2, K4, P2. (34 sts.)
2nd row K2, P4, K22, P4, K2.
3rd row P2, K4, P2, K18,

P2, K4, P2.
4th row K2, P4, K22, P4, K2.
5th row P2, C4F, P22, C4F, P2.
6th row As 4th row.
7th row P2, K4, P22, K4, P2.
8th row As 6th.
9th row As 7th.
10th row As 6th.
Rep 5th-10th rows once more, then 5th-8th rows once.
Keeping patt correct, inc one st at each end of next 4 rows. (42 sts.)
Work 43 rows in patt.
K 4 rows. Bind off.

Armhole edging
Using No.3 needles, with RS facing, pick up and K 25 sts evenly around armhole.
K 1 row. Bind off.
Work around other armhole in same way.

Finishing

Press lightly under a damp cloth with a warm iron.
Join side seams including armhole edgings. Press seams.

Cap

Using No.3 needles, cast on 72 sts.
1st row *K1, P1, rep from * to end.
Rep 1st row 3 times more.
5th row P to end.
6th row K to end.
Rep 5th and 6th rows once more.
9th row P3, *P up 1, P6, rep from * to last 3 sts, P up 1, P3. Work 5 rows without shaping.
15th row P3, *P up 1, P1, P up 1, P6, rep from * to last 4 sts, P up 1, P1, P up 1, P3.
Work 7 rows without shaping.
23rd row P2, *P2 tog, P1, P2 tog tbl, P4, rep from * to last 7 sts, P2 tog, P1, P2 tog tbl, P2. Work 5 rows without shaping.
29th row P1, *P2 tog, P1, P2 tog tbl, P2, rep from * to last 6 sts, P2 tog, P1, P2 tog tbl, P1. Work 3 rows without shaping.
33rd row *P2 tog, P1, P2 tog tbl, rep from * to last 5 sts, P2 tog, P1, P2 tog tbl.

Work 3 rows without shaping.
37th row *P2 tog, rep from * to end.
K1 row.
Break off yarn leaving 12in length. Draw yarn through rem sts and draw into circle. Join seam from center to cast-on edge. Make small pompon as shown in Crochet Know-how chapter 14, page 262 and sew to center.

Reversed stockinette stitch cap and waistcoat with cable panels (Note: Gregor's waistcoat is worn inside out to show what reversed cable stitch looks like) ►
The doll's wardrobe so far:
▼ *Shirt and shorts (page 262)*

▼ *Party dress and coat (page 322)*

▼ *Pullover and pants (page 482)*

Clematis in crochet

This pretty crocheted vest with a delicate lacy edging in a clematis flower pattern can be coordinated with a skirt and blouse or with full, flowing crêpe pants for after-six occasions.

The main portion of the bodice is worked in easy-to-do half doubles. The lace borders are worked separately and sewed on after the main bodice is completed.

Sizes

Directions are for 32in bust. The figures in brackets [] refer to the 34, 36, 38 and 40in sizes respectively.
Length down center back, 24in.

Gauge
6¼ sts and 4¾ rows to 1in over half doubles worked on No.D crochet hook.

Materials

3-ply fingering yarn 13[13:15:15:16] ounces
One No.D (3.00 mm) crochet hook

Back and fronts
(divided at armholes)

Using No.D crochet hook, ch177 [193:205:217:229].
Base row 1hdc into 3rd ch from hook, 1hdc into each ch to end. Turn. 176[192:204:216:228] sts.
Next row Ch2, 1hdc into each st to end, 1hdc into top of turning ch. Turn.
The last row forms patt and is rep throughout.
Continue in patt until work measures 14[13½:13½:13:13] in from beg.

604

Shape front edges
Next row Ss over one st, ch2, patt to last st. Turn.
Next row Ch2, patt to end. Turn. Rep last 2 rows 4 times more. 166[182:194:206:218] sts.

Divide for armholes and continue shaping front edge
Next row Ss over one st, ch2, patt 25[27:29:31:33] sts. Turn.
Continue on these 26[28:30:32:34] sts for right front.
Next row Ss over one st, ch2, patt to end. Turn.
Rep last row 7 times more. 14[16:18:20:22] sts.
This completes armhole shaping.
Next row Ch2, patt to end. Turn.
Next row Ss over one st, ch2, patt to end. Turn.
Rep last 2 rows 10[11:12:13:14] times more. 3[4:5:6:7] sts.
Continue without shaping until work measures 24in from beg. Fasten off.
With RS of work facing, skip next 12[16:18:20:22] sts, attach yarn to next st, ch2, patt 87[91:95:99:103] sts. Turn.
Continue on these 88[92:96:100:104] sts for back.
Next row Ss over one st, ch2, patt to last st. Turn.
Rep last row 7 times more, turning with ch2 on last row. 72[76:80:84:88] sts.
Continue without shaping until back measures same as right front.

Shape shoulders
Next row Ss over 6[7:8:7:8] sts, ch2, patt to end. Turn.

Rep last row once more.
Next row Ss over 7[7:7:8:8] sts, ch2, patt to end. Turn.
Rep last row 3 times more. Fasten off.
With RS of work facing, skip next 12[16:18:20:22] sts, attach yarn to next st, ch2, patt to last st. Turn. Continue on these 26[28:30:32:34] sts for left front.
Next row Ch2, patt to last st. Turn.
Next row Ss over one st, ch2, patt to last st. Turn.
Rep last 2 rows 3 times more. 14[16:18:20:22] sts.
Next row Ch2, patt to end. Turn.
Next row Ch2, patt to last st. Turn. Rep last 2 rows 10 [11:12:13:14] times more. 3[4:5:6:7] sts.
Continue without shaping until work measures same as right front. Fasten off.

Left front border

1st motif
** Ch6. Join with ss to first ch to form circle.
1st round Work 12sc into circle. Join with ss to first sc.
2nd round Ch3, (yoh, draw loop through st at base of these 3ch, yoh, draw loop through first 2 loops) 4 times, yoh, draw loop through all loops on hook (1 cluster made), *ch4, skip 1 st, work cluster in next st as follows: (yoh, draw loop through, yoh, draw loop through first 2 loops) 5 times, yoh, draw loop through all loops on hook, rep from * 4 times more, ch4, join with ss to top of first cluster.**
3rd round Ch3, (yoh, draw loop through top of first cluster, yoh, draw loop through first 2 loops) twice, yoh, draw loop through all loops on hook, ch3, (yoh, draw loop through top of same cluster, yoh, draw loop through first 2 loops) 3 times, yoh, draw loop through all loops on hook (double petal just made), ch3, 1sc in ch space, ch3, *work double petal in top of next cluster as follows: (yoh, draw loop

through top of cluster, yoh, draw loop through first 2 loops) 3 times, yoh, draw loop through all loops on hook, ch3, (yoh, draw loop through top of same cluster, yoh, draw loop through first 2 loops) 3 times, yoh, draw loop through all loops on hook, ch3, 1sc in ch space, ch3, rep from * all around. Join with ss in top of first cluster.
Fasten off.

2nd motif
Work as for 1st motif from ** to **.
Join motifs together in next round as follows:
Next round Ch3, (yoh, draw loop through top of first cluster, yoh, draw loop through first 2 loops) twice, yoh, draw loop through all loops on hook, ch3, (yoh, draw loop through top of same cluster, yoh, draw loop through first 2 loops) 3 times, yoh, draw loop through all loops on hook, ch3, 1sc in ch space, ch3, *work in top of next cluster as follows: (yoh, draw loop through top of cluster, yoh, draw loop through first 2 loops) 3 times, yoh, draw loop through all loops on hook, ch1, place 1st motif at back of work with WS together and join them by working 1sc in ch space between a double petal of 1st motif, ch1, (yoh, draw loop through top of same cluster on 2nd motif, yoh, draw loop through first 2 loops) 3 times, yoh, draw loop through all loops on hook, ch3, 1sc in ch space, ch3*, rep from * to * once more then complete round as for 1st motif.
Make another 9 motifs in the same way, joining 2 double petals together in 3rd round as before.

Work edges
With RS facing, attach yarn to double petal at side of 1st motif and work as follows:
1st round *2ss in ch space in center of double petal, ch1, 1hdc in next ch space, ch2, 1dc in next ch space, ch1,

▲ *Crochet vest with lace motif borders, elegant in white but equally effective in pastel or bright colors*

▼ *Detail of lace motif border*

1tr in each of next 2 ch spaces, ch1, 1dc in next ch space, ch2, 1hdc in next ch space, ch1, rep from * to last double petal along side edge, **2ss in ch space in center of double petal, ch2, 1tr in each of next 2 ch spaces, ch2, 2ss in next ch space, (ch1, 1hdc in next ch space) twice, ch2, 2ss in next ch space, ch2, 1tr in each of next 2 ch spaces, ch2**, rep from * to last double petal along other side, then work from ** to **. Join with ss. Turn.

With WS facing, work back as follows:

Next round Make bobble in next st as follows: (yoh, insert hook in st and draw a loop through) 4 times, yoh, draw loop through all loops on hook, (ch2, skip 1 st, make bobble) 3 times, (ch1, skip 1 st, make bobble) 3 times, (ch2, skip 1 st, make bobble) 3 times, *ch1, skip 1 st, make bobble, ch1, skip 2 sts, make bobble, rep from * along side edge, then work around corners as before, then rep from * along other side edge. Join

with ss to top of bobble. Fasten off.

Right front border

Work as given for left front border.

Finishing

Press each piece very lightly on WS under a damp cloth. With RS facing, sew borders to fronts neatly. Join shoulder seams. Press seams.
Work 2 rounds sc around each armhole. Fasten off.

Fabric stitch fantasia

Crochet Know-how 31

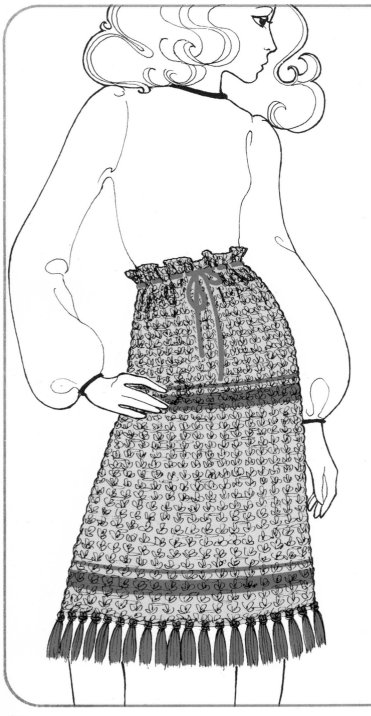

The same firm, close fabrics can be obtained with crochet stitches as can be with knitting stitches—it just depends on the size hook and the thickness of the yarn you select. The examples shown here are ideal for garments which require a hard-wearing fabric, such as coats, suits, jackets and skirts.

To make the attractive peasant skirt illustrated, simply work two strips of crochet, one for the skirt back and one for the front, using any of the fabric stitches in this chapter. Work in a single bright color or, for a striking effect, in horizontal stripes of contrasting colors. Join the two strips along the side edges, gather the waist on a cord and tie in front. Work a fringe around the hem.

Cluster stitch

Make a number of chains divisible by 3.

1st row. Into 3rd ch from hook work 2dc, skip 2ch, *1sc and 2dc into next ch, skip 2ch, rep from * to last st, 1sc in last st. Turn.

2nd row. Ch2, 2dc into first sc, *1sc and 2dc into each sc of previous row, rep from * ending with 1sc in turning ch. Turn.

The 2nd row forms pattern and is repeated throughout.

Claw stitch

Make a number of chains divisible by 2.

1st row. Into 4th ch from hook work 1dc, *skip 1ch, 2dc into next ch, rep from * to end.

2nd row. Ch3, *work 2dc between 2dc of previous row, rep from * to end. Turn.

The 2nd row forms pattern and is repeated throughout.

Elongated basket stitch

Make a number of chains divisible by 3, plus 1.

1st row. Into 2nd ch from hook work 1sc, 1sc into each ch to end. Turn.

2nd row. Ch2, 1sc into each sc to end. Turn.

3rd row. Ch3, 1dc into each of next 2sc, *(inserting hook in the space between one st and the next on first sc row, work 1dc drawing up a long loop) 3 times, 1dc into each of next 3sc, rep from * to end. Turn.

4th row. As 2nd.

5th row. Ch3, (inserting hook between one st and the next on row below previous row, work 1dc drawing up a long loop) twice, *1dc into each of next 3sc, (inserting hook between one st and the next on row below previous row, work 1dc drawing up a long loop) 3 times, rep from * to end. Turn.

Rows 2-5 form pattern and are repeated throughout.

Paving stone stitch

Make a number of chains divisible by 2.

1st row. Into 3rd ch from hook work 1dc, ch2, 1sc into next ch, *skip 2ch, 2dc into next ch, ch2, 1sc into next ch, rep from * to end. Turn.

2nd row. Ch2, *work 2dc, ch2 and 1sc into 2ch loop of previous row, rep from * to end, 1sc in turning ch. Turn.

The 2nd row forms pattern and is repeated throughout.

Straw stitch

Make a number of chains divisible by 5, plus 1.

1st row. Into 3rd ch from hook work 1sc, 1sc into each of next 3ch, *1dc into each of next 5ch, 1sc into each of next 5ch, rep from * to end. Turn.

2nd row. Ch3, 1dc into each of next 4sc, *1sc into each of next 5dc, 1dc into each of next 5sc, rep from * to end. Turn.

3rd row. Ch2, 1sc into each of next 4dc, *1dc into each of next 5sc, 1sc into each of next 5dc, rep from * to end. Turn.

Rows 2 and 3 form pattern and are repeated throughout.

▲*Cluster stitch, a particularly close fabric stitch*

▲*Claw stitch, a fairly firm fabric stitch suitable for lightweight jackets*

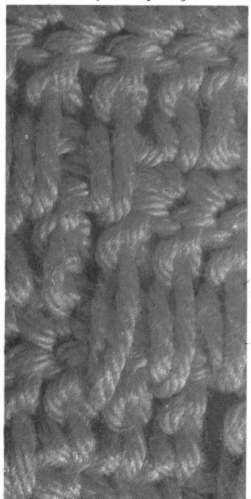

◄ *Elongated basket stitch*　　　　▲ *Paving stone stitch*　　　　▼ *Straw stitch*

Embroidery with braid and ribbon

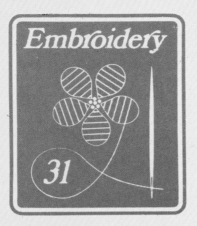

Braid embroidery is a simple form of appliqué. Dimension and texture are added by using ribbons, beads and sequins.

When braid embroidery is combined with other forms of appliqué and embroidery, the possible effects are many and varied. The richly raised finish is ideal for clothes, table linen and wall panels. When working braid embroidery on table linen, remember to position the design so that unworked areas are left for plates and glasses when the table is set.

Materials and yarns

This type of embroidery is worked with a narrow braid of wool, cotton or synthetic yarn. The width of braid you choose will depend on the final effect desired and can measure from $\frac{1}{4}$ inch to 2 inches.

The textures can be varied by the introduction of leather, suede, felt, plastic, cord, metallic yarn, beads or sequins, intermingling these with the braid. Ribbon creates a pretty effect, whether you use nylon, satin or velvet, and if you are very enthusiastic, you may want to make your own braids in crochet, knitting or macramé. If the braid is held down with a decorative stitch, the decoration is sewed in place with sewing thread, invisible thread or embroidery thread. Additional embroidery stitches are then used to add detail.

The background fabric should be a firmly woven material such as velvet, upholstery fabric or a strong linen.

Designs for braid embroidery

Designs should be basically simple. The technique lends itself well to modern geometric and abstract designs formed by straight lines or free flowing curves. Detail can be added in the form of embroidery stitches or beading.

Method of working

Trace the design onto the right side of the background fabric (see Embroidery chapter 4, page 68). Sew the outline braid around the design (see diagram), using a simple running stitch or small backstitch about an $\frac{1}{8}$ inch long and worked at $\frac{3}{8}$ inch intervals along the center of the braid. Machine stitching can be used provided that the braid is first basted firmly in place.

When working around corners, ease the braid so that the inside edge is slightly fuller than the outside one. The curves are then pressed into shape to lie smooth and flat.

Effects with braid

Braid flowers are made by looping the braid into the shape of individual petals (see illustration). Secure the end of each loop with several stitches.

The centers of these looped flowers are decorated with embroidery stitches.

▲ *Ribbons and braids can be used in a variety of ways for pictures and panels*

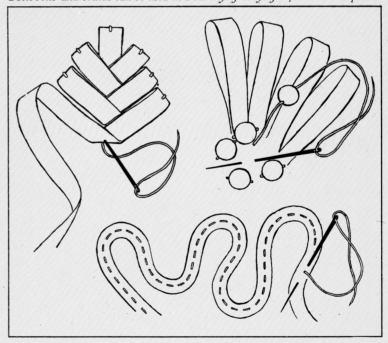

▲ *Sewing the braid, and detail showing how stalk of wheat is worked*

Stalks of wheat are quick to make. Mark a center line on the background and work a line of double loops going to right and left of this center line, sewing the loops down at the center as you work. A single line of outline stitch forms the beard and smaller ones are made between the ends of the loops.

Complete the design by couching lengths of cord, or work embroidery stitches for stems and leaves.

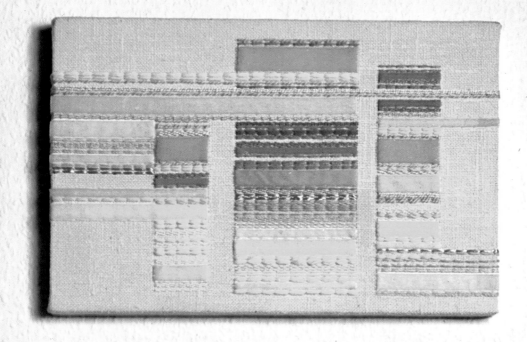

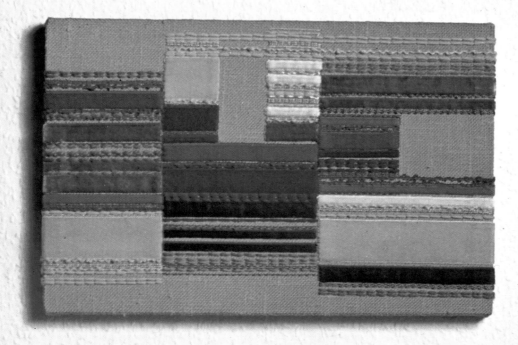

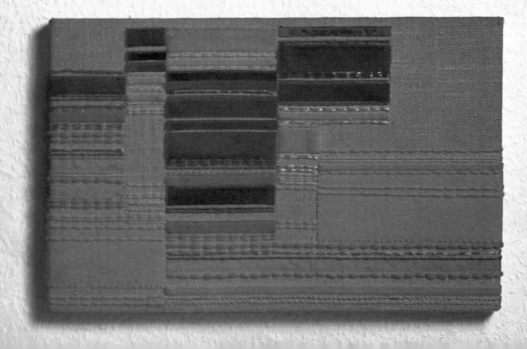

Seasons in color

These three panels show an interesting modern interpretation of braid embroidery using a variety of widths of velvet ribbon mounted on heavy dress linen. They form part of a set of four, each measuring 10 inches by 15 inches. The panels depict the four seasons and the three pictured here are (from top to bottom) spring, summer and autumn. The background color in each panel relates in general terms to the season.

Yellow stands for spring with the joyous colors of crocuses, daffodils, jasmine, pink hyacinths and tulips, all blending with the more subtle shades of lilac.

Green represents summer with its green grass, trees and red flowers, bright and clear as on a midsummer's day.

Pink brings to mind autumn sunsets and complements the richness of the browns which suggest dying leaves and dark wet roofs.

However, only the color categories were suggested by each season. The individual shades were dictated by working them together as a scheme within each panel and it is the use of some form of pink in each panel which unites them.

The main object of the panels is to create an experiment in color, and the design, materials and stitchery are simple to avoid detracting from this. While the various aspects of the seasons influence the colors, it is the rectangular outlines of modern architecture which inspire the symmetry of the design.

Only two stitches are used—couching and outline stitch. Plastic raffia, pearl cotton, knitting wool and 6-strand embroidery floss are couched in their own color of mercerized sewing thread so that only indentations are seen.

The couching stitches are placed exactly in line with one another throughout the rows to follow through the idea of stark simplicity. All the ends of the couched threads are taken to the back of the work.

Filling in on canvas

There are many needlepoint stitches which, in addition to having unique characteristics of their own, create fascinating textures when repeated over large areas. This can be particularly useful when creating pictures, because you can use the textures to suggest the composition of the actual subject. For example, fern stitch could represent water and Roman bricking could be used for a stone building.

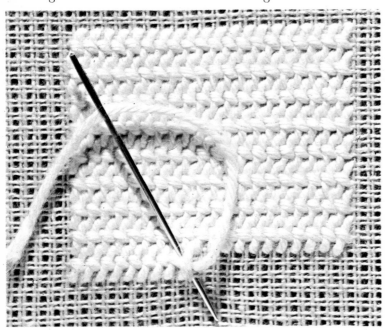

Knot stitch: working the second stage

Top: Romanian or Roman stitch, stage 1   *Bottom: stage 2*

As well as adding these stitches to your Harvest Fields sampler (Needlepoint chapter 4, page 92), you can use them for backgrounds. Where gaps occur around the outline of motifs, fill them in with tent stitch. The interesting textures of these stitches make them suitable for use over fairly large areas such as pillows or chair seats, and with an imaginative choice of color the effect can be made even more exciting. Compare Roman bricking shown here with the same stitch, illustrated in Needlepoint 1, p. 18. Worked in pinks and mauves, it takes on a completely new look. The use of different yarns such as metallic threads or raffia instead of wool will also make the stitches look different.

An interesting idea for another sampler would be to choose varying tones of a light color in different yarns to show the texture of the stitches to the best advantage—white, a rich shocking pink or a brilliant acid green.

N.B. The stitches are illustrated on double-weave canvas to show clearly how each stitch is made, but to insure a close covering of the canvas, remember to work them on single-weave canvas.

Knot stitch
This slanting stitch is worked over three threads of canvas and caught down with a small slanting stitch across the center of the stitch. The rows are interlocking.

Romanian or Roman stitch
This stitch consists of two rows, linked with a row of stitches worked in a similar way to outline stitch.

Work from left to right, and work each stitch from the top down over six threads and then work the central crossbar over the stitch working from right to left, one hole on each side of the long stitch. Complete the row in this manner.

To complete the stitch, a dividing row of outline stitch is worked from right to left, moving one hole to the left and two back all the way. This dividing row can be worked in the same color as the main stitch, or in a contrasting color or yarn. On double-weave canvas you can create an extremely pretty effect by working the main stitch over narrow strips of ribbon.

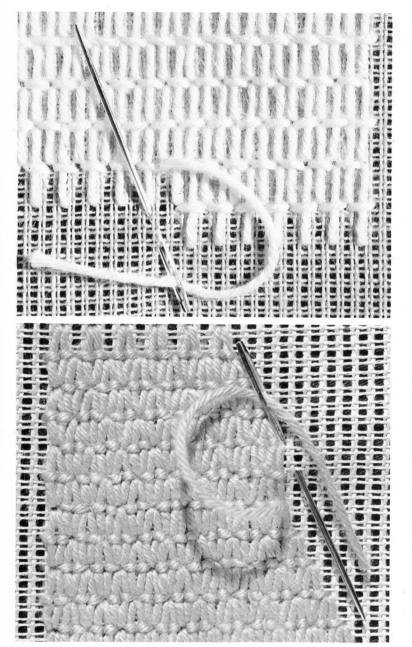

Top: Roman bricking   *Bottom: French stitch*

Top: Fern stitch   *Bottom: Rococo stitch*

Roman bricking

This is an interesting variation of Romanian stitch which gives a rich braiding effect.

Work in the same manner as Romanian stitch but move from right to left and take the crossbar from left to right.

The second row is worked in the same way from right to left, but interlock the stitches by bringing out the first stitch from the same hole as the crossing stitch of the previous row.

French stitch

This very closely textured stitch is worked in diagonal rows from top left to bottom right. It makes a most attractive pattern for a background or for incorporating into a design.

Work the main stitch from the bottom up over four threads, then make a central crossbar over it from right to left. Repeat the long stitch in the same holes and then work the crossbar from left to right, starting from the same hole as the previous crossbar.

Move down four holes to start the next stitch.

Fern stitch

This stitch is worked in downward vertical rows.

Start from the top left of the work. Insert the needle 2 holes down and 2 across and come out again one hole to the left. Insert the needle 2 holes up and 2 across and come out again one hole below the starting point of the previous stitch.

Continue down the length of the row and work the next one immediately alongside.

Rococo stitch

This stitch gives an attractive star-like pattern and makes a good background stitch.

Work as for Romanian stitch, working either 3 or 4 long stitches all from the same holes but held apart by the crossbars as shown in the picture.

To start the second stitch bring the needle out 4 holes along from the starting point of the first stitch and fit the second row in between the sections of the first row.

611

Scarf and beret set in daisywork

A pretty and practical fashion accessory, made on a Crazy Daisy Winder, this warm scarf and beret set will daisy-up cold, dull days.

Measurements
Scarf: 85in long by 7½in wide
Beret: 9½in across top, to fit average adult head

Materials you will need
One Hero Crazy Daisy Winder (2in diameter)
One No.D (3.00 mm) crochet hook
Sports yarn (2oz pull skeins)

Scarf: 3 skeins A, red
       1 skein B, white
Beret: 1 skein A, red
       1 skein B, white

Working the daisies
Using the Crazy Daisy Winder, make round daisies working two windings for the petals, using a single thread for overcasting an open center and working a lock stitch edging (see Daisy Work chapter 2).

Scarf

Using A, make a chain of 45 daisies, joining them as they are worked (see Daisy Work chapter 2, page 214).
Using B, make a chain of 46 daisies. Oversew to the previous chain, positioning the second daisy between the first two of the previous chain so that this row is half a daisy longer at each end.
Using A, make a chain of 47 daisies. Oversew to the previous chain so that this row is another half daisy longer at each end.
Using B, make a chain of 46 daisies. Oversew to previous chain so that this row is half a daisy shorter.
Using A, make a chain of 45 daisies. Oversew to the previous chain so that this row is half a daisy shorter.

Beret

Using A, make one daisy for center.
Using B, make a chain of 6 daisies to form a circle by leaving 2 petals free on the inner edge and 6 on the outer edge. Oversew around central daisy.
Using A, make a chain of 12 daisies to form a circle by leaving 2 petals free as before on inner edge of every alternate daisy and 4 on the inner edge of every other alternate daisy. Oversew to previous round, positioning every second daisy between two of the previous round.
Using B, make a chain of 18 daisies to form a circle by leaving petals free as on previous round for inner edge, but at the same time work the lock stitch joining to unite three petals instead of the usual two. Oversew to previous round so that the first daisy is positioned between the first and second of the previous round, the second between the second and third of the previous round, and the third on the outside edge of the third of the previous round. Continue all around in this way.
Using A, make a straight chain of 12 daisies joining the first to the last. Oversew to the previous round, positioning the first daisy between the first and second of the previous round, the second between the third and fourth of the previous round, the third between the fourth and fifth, the fourth between the sixth and seventh, continuing in this way all around.
Make a crochet band by working 1sc in each free petal and 1sc in the join between daisies. Continue in rounds until band measures 1½in. Fasten off.

▼*Close-up showing the end shaping of the scarf*

▼*Close-up showing the positioning of the beret daisies*

Dealing with disasters

Successful stain removal depends upon two factors: treating the stain or spot as soon as possible after it has occured, and using cleaning methods and chemicals which have a sensible relationship to the staining agent.

Stains left on fabrics for any length of time can become more difficult to remove, and emergency treatment can often make stain removal easier. For instance, stains originating from tea, coffee, fruit juices and most alcoholic drinks must be treated with water at once; grease spots should be dusted with talcum powder or chalk. The information in this chapter relates to the removal of small spots and stains.

Types of stains
The three main types of stains are: those originating from substances based on water (for example, fruit juices, alcoholic drinks) which, in the majority of cases, can be removed with water; those which contain oil, waxes and greases (butter, candle grease) and require the use of dry solvents to effect their removal; stains originating from chemical substances (paints, lacquers, glues), which are best treated by professional cleaners.

Three types of fluids are used mainly in the treatment of stains: liquid oxidizing bleaches (hydrogen peroxide and sodium hypochlorite); solvents (acetone, rubbing alcohol, turpentine, carbon tetrachloride) and liquid detergents.

The chart shows the dilution of recommended stain removal fluids. Remember to be careful when using them and be sure to follow the instructions.

Using bleaches
Bleaches are used for removing the residue of stains from fabrics after they have been soaked. (Stains originating from beer, coffee, blood, fruit juices, and similar substances fall into this category.) The treatment of these stains (see stain removal chart) involves removing the surface deposits, then soaking the fabric with water or water and detergent, and afterward, applying a bleaching agent.

Two main types of liquid bleaches are available for domestic use—hydrogen peroxide and sodium hypochlorite (laundry bleach, recognizable by smell). Diluted hydrogen can be used safely on all fabrics where the colors will withstand bleach treatment. Sodium hypochlorite bleach, even when diluted, MUST NEVER be used on articles made of wool, silk or rayon, or fabrics which have been given a flameproof or crease-resistant finish.

Most brand-name detergent powders contain sodium perborate, a powdered form

614

of oxidizing bleach, which can often be used to remove stains from fabrics or articles capable of being washed at a high temperature (176°F, 80°C).

Do's and don'ts with bleaches
Always test for colorfastness on an inside hem or an inconspicuous part of the garment before using bleach. Place the area to be tested between two pieces of white cloth and iron warm.

If no color transfer occurs, the fabric can be considered colorfast, and the bleach treatment can be used safely.

Always rinse the fabric thoroughly with water to remove all traces of bleach after treating a stain, and then wash normally.

Never use undiluted bleach on any article.

Never use a bleaching treatment on any garment labeled "dry clean only."

Using solvents
Solvents are used on stains which originate from oil or have a grease base, such as butter, lipstick, oil, paint, tar, and substances such as nail polish and chewing gum. Most solvents are highly inflammable and those which can be purchased for domestic use are shown in the dilution chart. Solvents and chemicals marked on the chart with a red skull and crossbones should be handled with extreme caution.

Do's and don'ts with solvents and chemicals
Never use solvents near a naked flame (and this includes lighted cigarettes).

Never use solvents in a closed room or a confined space.

Never use acetone on articles made of or containing acetate or triacetate rayons.

Never apply a second, different solvent or chemical until the first has dried out and the fabric has been rinsed with water.

Never use an iron to dry solvent-wet fabric. Leave the solvent to dry by evaporation.

Always test fabric colorfastness, especially when treating printed fabrics.

Equipment needed for removing stains
Preplanning your stain removal equipment will mean that sudden accidents need not result in permanent damage to clothes and household items. Keep all your equipment together in a cool place, on a high shelf if possible, away from the reach of children. Solvents and chemicals should always be stored away from open fires, stoves, and naked lights. If poisonous chemicals form part of your stain removing equipment, the storage place must be a cupboard which can be securely locked.

Stain-removing liquids
The various solvents, chemicals and detergents discussed in this chapter are best stored in 1-ounce and 2-ounce glass dropper bottles. Pharmacists can supply these bottles, the most suitable having a combined safety and dropper stopper which allows liquid to be applied one drop at a time. They can be purchased in a clear and also tinted glass so that reagents which react to light can be stored safely. Your druggist will advise which kind you need when you purchase stain removing liquids.

Label bottles clearly and give the labels a coating of clear varnish to protect them. Bottles containing liquids which are shown on the chart as dangerous, or needing special care in their use, should be identified clearly on the label. A large red cross, for danger, is a good way of marking the label.

Useful tools
Some stains leave a hard deposit on the surface of the fabric—chocolate, blood, egg white and ice cream each leave a residue.

This deposit has to be removed from the fabric before the stain can be properly treated. A bone spatula, flat and smooth at one end with a blunt point at the other, is ideal for breaking up the stain residue and, if used carefully, will not damage the fabric. Stain removing fluids should be applied to fabrics very gently. You will find this easier to do if your equipment includes one or two small sticks of wood with padded tips and some bristle brushes. Cotton swabs, available from druggists are effective for applying solvents to very small stains. For treating larger stains, pad the end of a wood stick with a piece of cotton, cover it with a scrap of cotton fabric and tie the pad to the stick securely with cotton thread.

Artists' natural bristle paint brushes are ideal for stain removal. Choose brushes with a flat edge, about $\frac{1}{4}$ inch to $\frac{3}{8}$ inch wide. A fairly stiff bristle is suitable for working on woolens and a soft bristle for delicate fabrics. It is advisable to keep a white bristle brush for working on white fabrics.

An absorbent pad is necessary during stain spotting operations to soak up the dissolved stain and the excess solvent or chemical. Terrycloth is ideal for this purpose. Cut a piece of terrycloth 36 inches long and 18 inches wide and fold it into a pad 9 inches by 9 inches. Cover the terrycloth pad with a piece of clean white cotton. The pad should be laundered frequently.

Your stain removal equipment should also include small pieces of muslin for "feathering out"—the term used for gently spreading the area of the solvent—and a small piece of chamois leather, ideal for soaking up excess water quickly.

Removing a stain

Identify the source of the stain, taking emergency action as soon as possible after the accident has occurred. Emergency measures include applying water to water soluble stains and talcum powder or chalk to grease stains.

Check the stain chart on the next page and prepare all the equipment you need, including a large glass or china bowl if a small area of fabric requires soaking.

The stain removal chart on the following page gives stage-by-stage instructions for dealing with specific stains on both washable fabrics and those which can only be dry-cleaned. Make sure that you proceed exactly according to the instructions given.

Where the chart instructions indicate that a stain is to be "treated" or "spotted" with a chemical or solvent, place the article with the stained side downward on the cotton-covered terrycloth pad. Working from the back of the stain, apply the solvent gently, working in a ring just outside the stain and proceeding toward the center, using more solvent as you work. Persevere gently with the treatment—repeated, mild applications are often more successful than a drastic process involving a high concentration of chemicals. Some treatments suggest that the stains should be flushed out with solvent after the stain has been treated. This means using a drop or two of clean solvent on the site of the stain to remove any particles of matter which may have become trapped between the fabric fibers.

Do's and don'ts in stain removal

Never attempt to treat fabrics which have special finishes or laminated or foam back construction.

If the cause of a stain is unknown, always use water first. If water is unsuccessful, dry the fabric and try recommended solvents. Oxidizing bleaches and acids should only be used as a last resort.

Do not attempt stain removal with solvents if garments are badly soiled or a ring will develop which may be difficult to remove. Take the garment, untreated, to a professional dry cleaner and tell him the origin of the stain.

Always use solvents and chemicals with extreme caution, in the recommended strengths, and be careful not to let drips fall on other parts of the garment.

Chemical	Recommended concentration	Notes
Acetic acid	1 part to 4 parts of water	Never use full strength
Acetone	As purchased	Alternative to amyl acetate
Alcohol	As purchased	Rubbing alcohol
Ammonia	1 part to 5 parts of water	DANGEROUS at full strength
Amyl Acetate	As purchased	Alternative to acetone
Borax	1 tablespoonful to $\frac{1}{2}$ pint water	Very weak alkali which can be used on delicate colors as an alternative to ammonia
Cleaning fluid	As purchased	Must not be used in a confined space
Detergent—powder	Use as recommended by the manufacturers	Any brand
Detergent—liquid	1 part to 4 parts of water or at normal wash strength	Neutral type
Glycerine	As purchased	Stain lubricant in wet treatments
Hydrochloric acid	1 part to 3 parts of water	DANGEROUS—can be used as an alternative to oxalic acid
Hydrogen peroxide	1 part of 10 volume to 4 parts of water	Never use full strength. Soak in solution for up to 12 hours. Rinse out thoroughly
Oil of eucalyptus	As purchased	
Oxalic Acid	1 plastic teaspoonful to one pint of water (plastic or glass container only)	VERY DANGEROUS POISON. NOT TO BE USED ON WOOL OR SILK
Sodium hypochlorite	For small stains: $\frac{1}{2}$ fluid oz to 2 pints cold water. For large stains: $\frac{1}{2}$ fluid oz to $2\frac{1}{2}$ gallons of cold water	Treatment must not continue for more than 5 minutes. Rinse out thoroughly Soak the entire article for not more than 15 minutes. Rinse out thoroughly

Follow the stain treatment instructions on the next pages stage-by-stage in the order given. Dilute chemicals to the strengths given in the dilution chart and always rinse out one chemical before applying the next.

Stain removal methods should not be attempted on large stains; refer these to a professional dry cleaner. It is recommended that thin rubber gloves be worn while handling chemicals, bleaches and solvents.

•Stain removal chart•

Stain	Washable white or fast dry articles	Colored, delicate or dry clean only articles
Beer	**Cottons**—wash at high temperature and clear residual traces with sodium hypochlorite bleach. **Wool and Silk** 1. Spot with acetic acid (vinegar). 2. Rinse out with water. 3. Hydrogen peroxide bleach. Soak if necessary.	1. Apply cold water. 2. Spot with acetic acid—rinse well.
Blood	1. Brush off surface deposits. 2. Soak in hand-warm solution of detergent. 3. **Cottons**—treat with oxalic acid—rinse well, then if necessary, use sodium hypochlorite bleach. **Wool and Silk**—treat with hydrochloric acid—rinse out and then bleach with hydrogen peroxide if necessary.	1. Treat with cold water containing ten drops of liquid detergent. 2. Apply acetic acid (vinegar)—rinse out thoroughly. 3. Refer persistent staining to professional treatments.
Butter	1. Apply cleaning fluid. 2. Flush out with excess solvent.	Same treatment.
Chocolate	1. Soak in warm detergent solution. 2. **Cotton**—sodium hypochlorite bleach (see dilution chart). **Wool**—hydrogen peroxide bleach (see dilution chart).	1. Treat with lukewarm water. 2. Treat with borax solution—rinse out thoroughly. Apply acetic acid—rinse out thoroughly.
Coffee	1. Soak in liquid detergent solution over night. 2. Wash in normal way. **If stain persists** **Cottons**—treat with sodium hypochlorite bleach. **Wool and silk**—treat with hydrogen peroxide (see dilution chart)	1. Treat with lukewarm water. 2. Apply acetic acid (vinegar)—rinse out thoroughly. **If stain persists** Use hydrogen peroxide if color permits, or refer stains to professional treatment.
Clear oil	Apply cleaning fluid.	Flush out with excess solvent.
Dyes	**Cotton** 1. Treat with rubbing alcohol made alkaline with ammonia (5 drops to about $\frac{1}{4}$ cup of alcohol). 2. Wash in normal way. **Wool and Silk** 1. Treat with hydrogen peroxide bleach—rinse out. 2. Wash in normal way.	Domestic treatments not advised.
Egg (yolk and white)	1. Remove surface deposits with dry brush. 2. Soak in detergent solution. 3. Wash in normal way.	1. Remove surface deposits. 2. Apply cold water. 3. Residual traces may respond to diluted ammonia if color permits.
Fruit juices	If fabric is suitable, wash at a high temperature. 1. Treat other fabrics with a weak solution of liquid detergent followed by normal wash. 2. **Cottons**—residual traces, treat with sodium hypochlorite bleach. **Wool and Silk**—treat with hydrogen peroxide.	1. Treat with cold water and liquid neutral detergent. 2. Refer extensive or residual stains to professional treatment.
Grass	1. Treat with rubbing alcohol. 2. Wash in normal way. 3. Bleach with hydrogen peroxide.	1. Treat with rubbing alcohol and refer to professional treatment.
Grease	1. Apply cleaning fluid. 2. Flush out with excess solvent.	Same treatment.
Hair spray	Treat with amyl acetate BUT NOT ON ACETATE OR TRIACETATE RAYONS.	Same treatment.
Ice Cream	1. Remove surface deposit with dry brush. 2. Treat with cleaning fluid or perchloroethylene. 3. Wash in normal way.	1. Remove surface deposits. 2. Dab with a weak solution of liquid detergent—rinse and dry. 3. Apply solvent—rinse with excess solvent.

Stain	Washable white or fast dry articles	Colored, delicate or dry clean only articles
Ink (ball point)	1. Treat with rubbing alcohol until no more color can be removed. 2. Wash in normal way.	1. Treat with rubbing alcohol. 2. Refer residual stains to professional treatment.
Ink (blue black)	Treat as for Metallic stains.	Same treatment.
Lipstick	1. Treat with perchloroethylene or cleaning fluid—dry. 2. Treat with liquid detergent—rinse. 3. Wash in normal way.	1. Treat with dry solvent. 2. Apply oil of eucalyptus. 3. Rinse with dry solvent.
Metallic stains	**Cottons** 1. Soak in oxalic acid solution (see dilution chart). 2. Rinse well. 3. Wash in normal way. **Wool and silk** 1. Spot treat with hydrochloric acid (see dilution chart). 2. Rinse well. 3. Wash in normal way.	DO NOT ATTEMPT DOMESTIC TREATMENTS.
Milk	1. Soak in a solution of detergent. 2. Wash in normal way.	1. Treat with cold water only. 2. Refer residual traces to professional treatment.
Nail polish	Treat as for hair spray BUT NOT ON ACETATE OR TRIACETATE RAYONS.	
Paint (emulsion)	1. Remove by soaking in cold water. 2. Wash in normal way.	1. Treat with cold water. 2. Refer residual traces to professional treatment.
Paint (oil)	1. Treat with cleaning fluid. 2. Flush out with excess solvent—allow to dry. 3. Wash in normal way.	Treat with dry solvent and then refer to professional treatment.
Scorch	1. Brush off surface marks. 2. Wash in normal way. 3. Bleach with hydrogen peroxide. INTENSE SCORCH MARKS MUST BE CONSIDERED PERMANENT.	1. Brush off surface marks. 2. Treat with warm borax solution (one tablespoonful to $\frac{1}{2}$ pint water). 3. Rinse well. 4. Bleach with hydrogen peroxide if colors are fast.
Shoe polish	1. Treat with dry solvent—allow to dry. 2. Soak in liquid detergent. 3. Wash in normal way.	1. Apply dry solvent—allow to dry. 2. Treat with glycerine. 3. Rinse in cold water.
Tar	1. Soften stain with margarine or butter. 2. Apply dry solvent. 3. Repeat treatments until marks are removed. 4. Wash in normal way.	1. Soften with margarine. 2. Apply dry solvent—rinse with excess solvent. 3. Refer residual stains to professional treatment.
Tea	1. Soak in liquid detergent solution. 2. Wash at a high temperature if fabric permits or treat with hydrogen peroxide bleach.	1. Treat with cold water. 2. Treat with diluted liquid detergent. 3. Bleach with hydrogen peroxide if color permits.
Wine	1. Soak in liquid detergent solution. 2. Wash in normal way. **Residual traces** 3. **Cotton**—sodium hypochlorite bleach. **Wool and Silk**—hydrogen peroxide bleach.	1. Apply cold water. 2. Treat with water and liquid detergent. 3. Bleach with hydrogen peroxide if color permits. 4. Residual stains to professional treatment.
Urine	1. Soak in liquid detergent. 2. Wash in normal way. 3. Treat residual stains with acetic acid (vinegar)—rinse well. 4. Treat with dilute ammonia. 5. Rewash.	1. Apply cold water. 2. Treat with acetic acid (vinegar)—rinse. 3. Treat with dilute ammonia. 4. Bleach with hydrogen peroxide if color permits.

617

Making the kilt

Dress-making 31

The previous chapter covered the preparations for kilt-making—how to work out the pleating, calculate yardage and choose a suitable fabric. In this chapter you will find full instructions for making a short kilt for a 23 inch maximum skirt length. The diagram shows you the pleating sequence at a glance and you can easily substitute your own working measurements where they differ from those given. If you have decided to make the floor length kilt—an ideal hostess skirt for wintertime entertaining—from the pattern shown in Dressmaking 30, page 596, then the know-how tips in this chapter are invaluable.

Preparing to pleat

Study figure 1, which is the pleating diagram. You will notice that there is an inverted pleat at the inner edge of the upper front panel. This is an extra pleat not accounted for in the pleat number (allowance was made for it in the 5 inches added for finishing the upper front panel, when calculating yardage). The inverted pleat enables the panel to lie flat and hang well. The pleat sequence for the kilt remains the same for all sizes apart from the measurement for the panels and the number of pleats. The pleating diagram indicates a left-hand fastening. For right-hand fastening, simply reverse the reading of the diagram.

Making the kilt

Cutting. Prepare the fabric for cutting as for the child's pleated skirt in Dressmaking chapter 13, page 256. Measure and mark the skirt lengths across the fabric, add hem and waist seam allowances and cut.

Making the hem. Make the hem before pleating, leaving 3 inches to each side of the seam(s) just basted. Press.

Pleating. With the fabric right side up and following figure 1, mark all the pleat lines, seamlines and edges with basting. Also mark the center front on both panels. Where the fabric is to be joined, finish with a half pleat depth and seam allowance and start the next section with a seam allowance followed by a half pleat depth.

Starting with the left panel, pleat from left to right pinning as for tailored pleats (see Dressmaking chapter 15, page 294). Make the inverted pleat by folding the upper front panel edge to meet the fold of the last pleat.

You are now ready to baste the pleats. Since the skirt is fitted from the hipline into the waist, baste each pleat from hipline to hem only and leave the top pinned for tapering.

Stitching the seams. Join the skirt sections, making sure as you baste and stitch each seam that it forms the inside crease of the pleat. Finish the hem at the base of each seam. (See the side seam for the child's pleated skirt, Dressmaking chapter 13.)

Tapering the pleats

The chart here shows you a simple way of calculating how much to taper each pleat.

What to do	For example 25in waist, 30in hip	For your own use
1. Add 2in ease to the waist measurement.	25in + 2in = 27in	....in + 2in = ...in
2. Find the difference between this figure and the hip measurement plus ease (3in).	33in—27in = 6in	....in—.....in = ...in
3. Divide the amount equally by the number of pleats (don't forget the inverted pleat!)	6in ÷ 26 pleats = about ¼in for tapering each pleat	....in ÷ ....pleats = ...in

The dash lines indicated on figure 1 show you how to taper the pleats. Roll under the edge of each pleat and bring it to meet the distance line of the next pleat. Be sure that each pleat runs back into the original line at the hips.

The fitting

Baste the top of the pleats firmly into position and press the pleats all the way down.

Cut a waistband the full length of the waist edge and baste it to the kilt.

Try on the kilt, and wrap the panels so that the center front lines meet. There must be enough ease for the panels to stay fully wrapped and not pull away from each other.

Use the fitting hints for the knife-pleated skirt in Dressmaking chapter 15, page 294 when you look at the pleats. You will find the skirt fitting guide in Dressmaking chapter 6, p. 116, useful, too. Mark any faults and correct them, unless you find you need to cut a curve for the waist—this should be done after you have stitched the pleats.

Finishing the kilt

Stitching the pleats. Remove the waistband and topstitch each pleat close to the edge from the waist to the hipline. Press.

Curving the waist. If you need to cut a waist curve, do so now. With the panels wrapped in position, fold the kilt in the center front lines and pin it together along the waistline. Curve the waist following the instructions in Dressmaking chapter 6. Baste the top of the pleats along the new seamline.

Fringing. To finish the upper front panel you can make your own fringe from the kilt material.

Cut a strip about 2 inches wide, a little longer than the length of the panel. Carefully lift out the threads from one edge until the fringe is about ¾ inch wide. Lay the fringed strip on the facing fold line of the upper panel as shown in figure 2 and stitch along this line. Trim, then hand-sew the inside raw edge to the facing.

Finishing the panels. Fold under the 3 inch facing on the upper front panel and the 1 inch turning on the edge of the under panel over the hem. Baste and hand-sew as shown in figure 3.

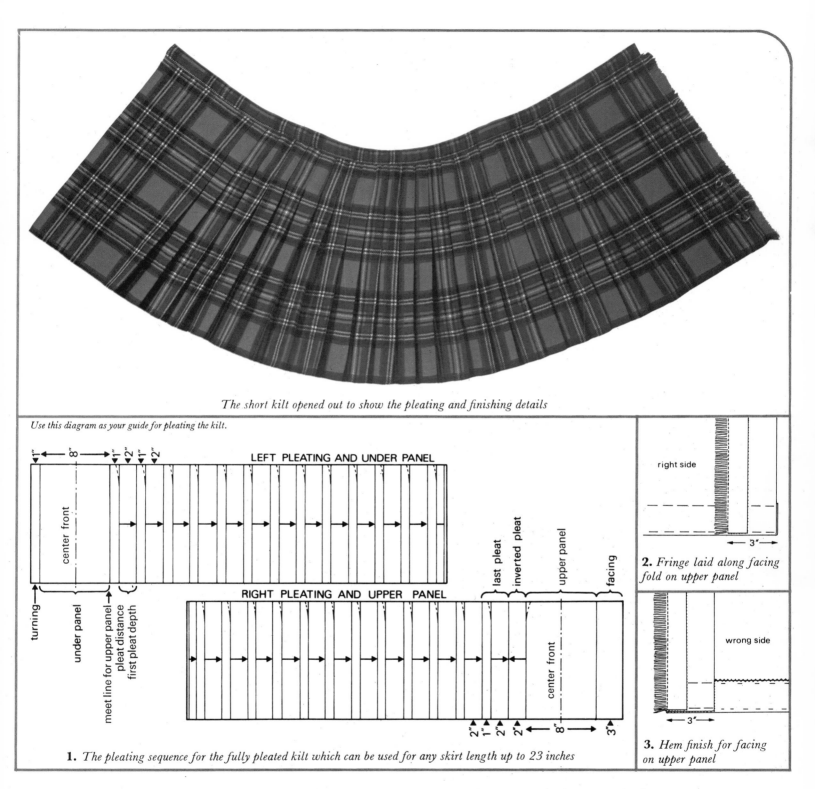

The short kilt opened out to show the pleating and finishing details

Use this diagram as your guide for pleating the kilt.

LEFT PLEATING AND UNDER PANEL

center front

turning

under panel

meet line for upper panel

pleat distance

first pleat depth

RIGHT PLEATING AND UPPER PANEL

last pleat

inverted pleat

upper panel

facing

center front

1. *The pleating sequence for the fully pleated kilt which can be used for any skirt length up to 23 inches*

right side

2. *Fringe laid along facing fold on upper panel*

wrong side

3. *Hem finish for facing on upper panel*

Fastening the waistband. Before you attach the waistband, consider the way you want the kilt to fasten. You can fasten it with a hook and eye, but if you want to be traditional, make a tab and buckle fastening—for this you can use the instructions for the buckle belt with pointed end in Dressmaking chapter 12, p. 236. The tab should project about 5 inches from the end of the waistband and there are two methods of attaching it, depending on the type of waistband you are making.

Method 1. If you are making a waistband with an elasticized back, the tab must be attached before you finish the end of the waistband. Make the tab a fraction narrower than the waistband, insert the raw edge into the end of the waistband on the upper front panel, then stitch twice across the end to secure it.

Method 2. If you are making a plain waistband, cut the tab slightly longer than 5 inches and make both ends pointed. Lay one pointed end onto the end of the waistband and topstitch neatly, following the shape of the point.

For both methods, the buckle can be stitched straight onto the waistband in line with the tab, or you can make a belt end for it and then sew it securely to the waistband. Use strong hooks and eyes or a trouser hook and bar on the under panel to hold the wrap in position.

Fashion Flair

Bright on white

White dresses are cool for summer, but to prevent the look from becoming positively icy it is a worthwhile fashion touch to add an embroidered contrast. The elegant, stylized design is shown here in a charted pattern and can easily be worked in cross stitch, blocks or bands of satin stitch, or even in square eyelets.

1. *The seaming of this dress is defined by the pattern which is taken across the yoke seam and down the front seams which lead into the pockets.*
2. *The 'V'-neck and front fastening of this dress are given a vest-like look.*
3. *Use the pattern for a feminine sleeve, edging the embroidery, neckline, side seams and cuffs with braid.*
4. *The design gives a bold look to a square neckline and huge patch pockets.*

Creative Hint. Always work the embroidery onto the garment pieces before joining them. You will then be working on flat surfaces, handling the minimum amount of fabric.

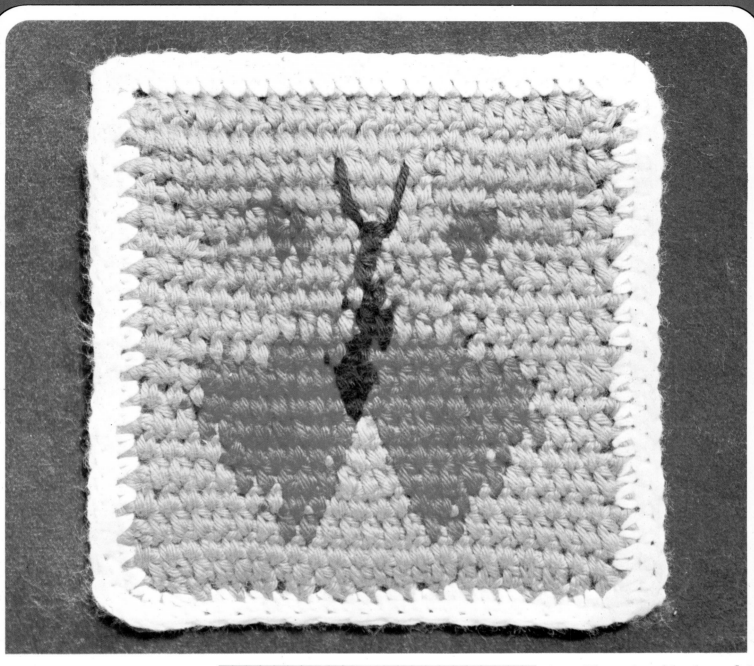

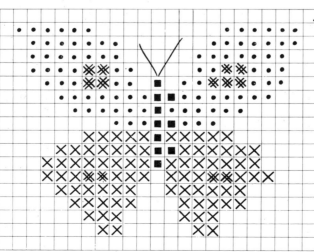

Pattern Library

Flutter by with a butterfly! Crochet Know-how 32 (page 622), 33 (page 646) and 34 (page 666) deal with jacquard motifs, working from a chart. Use attractive design to brighten up a plain crocheted sweater, working butterfly motif into the pattern or using design for a pocket. This example is shown worked in single crochet. For a colorful mat or potholder, finish edges in a contrasting color, choosing any of the edgings from Crochet Know-how 10 (p. 188), 23 (p. 446).

Bobbles big and small

Variations of bobble stitch produce a wonderfully textured fabric and are shown to their best effect in combination with other traditional stitches in Aran knitting.

By working the bobbles in groups on a plain stockinette stitch background, you can achieve an interesting, raised pattern suitable for almost any type of garment. The cardigan illustrated in this chapter shows groups of bobbles worked into a diamond shape and featured as decorative panels on the front of an otherwise simple cardigan.

To work a small bobble

Cast on a number of stitches divisible by 6, plus 5 stitches. For example 36 (i.e. 6 × 6) + 5 = 41 stitches. Beginning with a knit row, work two rows stockinette stitch.

1st row. K2 sts, work a bobble by knitting 5 times into next st, first into the front then into the back alternately, and leaving last st on left-hand needle, slip st off left-hand needle leaving 5 sts on right-hand needle, pass 2nd, 3rd, 4th and 5th sts over first st and off right-hand needle to complete bobble, *K5 sts, make a bobble in 6th st as before, rep from * to last 2 sts, K2.

2nd row. P to end.

3rd row. *K5 sts, make a bobble in next st as before, rep from * to last 5 sts, K5.

4th row. P to end.

These 4 rows form pattern and are repeated throughout.

Alternated rib and bobble stitch

Cast on a number of stitches divisible by 9, plus 4.

1st row. *K4, P2, K1, P2, rep from * to last 4 sts, K4.

2nd row. *P4, K2, P1, K2, rep from * to last 4 sts, P4.

3rd row. *K4, P2, bobble 1 in K st, P2, rep from * to last 4 sts, K4.

4th row. As 2nd.

These 4 rows form pattern and are repeated throughout.

Zigzag bobble stitch

Cast on a number of stitches divisible by 4, plus 2.

1st row. P.

2nd row. K.

Repeat 1st and 2nd rows once more.

5th row. P1, *bobble 1, P3, rep from * to last st, P1.

6th row. K1, *K3, P1, rep from * to last st, K1.

7th row. P1, *P1, bobble 1, rep from * to last st, P1.

8th row. K1, *P1, K1, rep from * to last st, K1.

9th row. P1, *P2, bobble 1, P1, rep from * to last st, P1.

10th row. K1, *K1, P1, K2, rep from * to last st, K1.

These 10 rows form pattern and are repeated throughout.

Diagonal bobble stitch

Cast on a number of stitches divisible by 7.

1st row. *K2, P2, K1, P2, rep from * to end.

▲ *Method for working a small bobble—knit five times into one stitch*
▼ *Then slip the stitch off the left-hand needle*

▼ *Slip four stitches over the first stitch.*

2nd row. *K2, P1, K2, P2, rep from * to end.

3rd row. *K2, P2, bobble 1, P2, rep from * to end.

4th row. As 2nd.

5th row. P1, *K2, P2, bobble 1, P2, rep from * to last 6 sts, K2, P2, bobble 1, P1.

6th row. K1, P1, *K2, P2, K2, P1, rep from * to last 5 sts, K2, P2, K1.

7th row. P2, *K2, P2, bobble 1, P2, rep from * to last 5 sts, K2, P2, bobble 1.

8th row. P1, *K2, P2, K2, P1, rep from * to last 6 sts, K2, P2, K2.

9th row. Bobble 1, P2, *K2, P2, bobble 1, P2, rep from * to last 4 sts, K2, P2.

10th row. K2, P2, *K2, P1, K2, P2, rep from * to last 3 sts,

622

▲ *Alternated rib and bobble stitch*
▼ *Diagonal bobble stitch*

▲ *Zigzag bobble stitch*
▼ *Simple cardigan with front panels of grouped bobbles*

K2, P1.

11th row. P1, bobble 1, P2, *K2, P2, bobble 1, P2, rep from * to last 3 sts, K2, P1.

12th row. K1, P2, *K2, P1, K2, P2, rep from * to last 4 sts, K2, P1, K1.

13th row. P2, bobble 1, P2, *K2, P2, bobble 1, P2, rep from * to last 2 sts, K2.

14th row. P2, *K2, P1, K2, P2, rep from * to last 5 sts, K2, P1, K2.

15th row. K1, P2, bobble 1, P2, *K2, P2, bobble 1, P2, rep from * to last st, K1.

16th row. P1, *K2, P1, K2, P2, rep from * to last 6 sts, K2, P1, K2, P1.

Rows 3-16 form pattern and are repeated throughout.

Sleeveless skimmer

Make this pretty top to wear with suits, skirts and all kinds of pants.

Sizes
Directions are for 32in bust. The figures in brackets [] refer to the 34, 36 and 38in sizes respectively.
Length to back neck, 16¾[17:17¼:17½]in.

> **Gauge**
> 7 sts and 10 rows to 1in over stockinette stitch worked on No.3 needles.

Materials
3-ply fingering yarn 6[6:7:7] 1oz balls
One pair No.1 needles (or Canadian No.12)
One pair No.2 needles (or Canadian No.11)
One pair No.3 needles (or Canadian No.10)
One No.B (2.00 mm) crochet hook

Back

Using No.1 needles, cast on 125[131:137:143] sts.
Beg with a K row, work 4 rows st st.
1st patt row Using No.3 needles, K.
2nd patt row (wrong side) Using No.3 needles, K1, *K3 tog, before slipping sts off left-hand needle K into first st again, then K 2nd and 3rd sts tog, slip all 3sts onto right-hand needle—called K3 into 3—rep from * to last st, K1.
3rd patt row As 1st patt row.
4th patt row As 2nd patt row.
5th-14th patt rows Using No.2 needles and beg with a K row, work in st st.
Rep 1st-14th rows 6 times
624

more, then 1st-10th rows once.

Shape armholes
1st row Using No.2 needles, bind off 6[6:6:9] sts, K to end.
2nd row Using No.2 needles, bind off 6[6:6:9] sts, P to end.
3rd row Using No.2 needles, bind off 3 sts, K to end.
4th row Using No.2 needles, bind off 3 sts, P to end.
5th row Using No.3 needles, bind off 3 sts, K to end.
6th row Using No.3 needles, bind off 3 sts (1 st on right-hand needle), *K3 into 3, rep from * to last st, K1. 101[107:113:113] sts.
Rep 1st and 2nd patt rows throughout remainder of back.
Work without shaping until armholes measure 5¾[6:6¼:6½] in, ending with 2nd patt row.

Shape neck
1st row Keeping patt correct, work 34[37:37:37] sts, bind off center 33[33:39:39] sts, patt to end.
Complete this shoulder first.
Work 1 row.
**Bind off 3 sts at neck edge every other row 3 times.

Shape shoulder
Bind off 7 sts at arm edge; then 9 sts on next arm edge row; then 9[12:12:12] sts on arm edge row. **
With WS of work facing, attach yarn to rem sts for other shoulder and work 2 rows.
Complete as for first shoulder from ** to **.

Front

Work as given for back.

Finishing

DO NOT PRESS.
Join shoulder and side seams using a backstitch seam.
Turn first 5 st st rows at lower edge to WS and slip st in place.
Neck edging Using No.B crochet hook, with RS of work facing, work picot edging evenly around neck edge, *1sc, 1sc into next st, ch3, 1sc into same place as last sc, rep from * to end. Work edging around armholes in same way.

Alternative knitted picot edging
Neck edge Join left shoulder seam.
Using No.2 needles, with RS of work facing, pick up and K13 sts down right side of back neck, K33[33:39:39] sts from center back bound-off edge, pick up and K13 sts up left side of back and 13 sts down left side of front, K 33[33:39:39] sts from center front bound-off edge and pick up and K13 sts up right side of front. 118[118:130:130] sts. Work picot edge.*
K into front and back of next st, turn, K2, turn, bind off 6 sts, slip st on right-hand needle back on left-hand needle and rep from * until all sts have been worked off.
Armhole edging Join right shoulder seam.
Using No.2 needles, with RS of work facing, pick up and K92[96:100:104] sts and work as for neck edging.

Pretty, yet quick and easy to knit ▶
▼ Detail of the bodice stitch

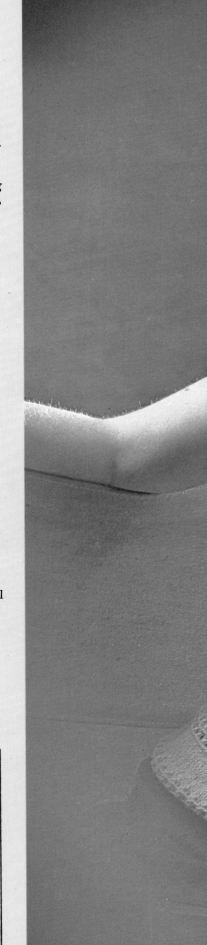

Ways with colorful crochet

Crochet Know-how 32

Jacquard effects can be obtained by using two or more colors. Working in several colors gives a close fabric, so use a hook one size larger than normal for the thickness of yarn.

Jacquard patterns give working directions in two ways, either by each row or by means of a chart. Where the former method is used, the background or main color will be given as main color A, the second color to be used will be given as contrast color B, and so on. If a chart is used, the main color is represented by a white, open square and the contrast color by a black dot. Subsequent colors would then be represented by different symbols, such as an X or O, and these would be shown in the directions. In the jacquard patterns illustrated, both methods are given so that you may become familiar with them.

Where the yarn has to be carried over 3 or more stitches in a pattern, it may be advisable in the following row to work over the yarn when working the central stitch or stitches of a block. To do this on the right side of the work, insert the hook through the stitch to be worked and under the loop of yarn on the wrong side, then work the stitch in the usual way. When working on the wrong side, insert the hook under the loop of yarn and then into the stitch to be worked and complete the stitch in the usual way. In the following pattern directions, this will be referred to as "working over main or contrast yarn." This prevents over-long loops at the back of the work and makes it easier to keep an even gauge.

Using contrast yarn in jacquard
When a contrast color has to be worked in during the work, the last 2 loops of the last stitch in the main color are drawn through with the yarn of the contrast color, always keeping the yarn on the wrong side of the work (see illustration).

Reverting to main color in jacquard
When reverting to the main color after working a group of stitches in a contrast color, the last 2 loops of the last stitch in the contrast color are drawn through with the yarn of the main color, always keeping the yarn on the wrong side of the work (see illustration).

Two-color square jacquard pattern
The pattern consists of multiples of 7 stitches, plus 6 and a turning chain. Ch22 using A.
1st row. Using A, work 1dc into 4th ch from hook, 1dc into each ch to end. Turn. 20dc.
2nd row. (right side) Join in contrast color B, ch2 in A and work 3rd ch in B, skip first dc, *using B work 1dc into each of next 4dc ending 4th dc by drawing A through last 2 loops on hook, using A work 1dc into each of next 3dc ending 3rd dc by drawing B through last 2 loops on hook, rep from * to last 5 sts, using B work 1dc into each of next 4dc ending 4th dc by drawing A through last 2 loops, 1dc into turning ch with A. Turn.

Top: working with the contrast yarn in jacquard crochet
Bottom: reverting to the main color yarn

3rd row. (wrong side) Keeping yarn not in use on wrong side ch2 in A, work 3rd ch in B, skip first dc, using B work 1dc into next dc, 1dc into each of next 2dc working over main color loop of row below, 1dc into next dc drawing A through last 2 loops, * using A work 1dc into next dc, 1dc into next dc working over contrast color loop of row below, 1dc into next dc drawing B through last 2 loops, using B work 1dc into next dc, 1dc into each of next 2dc working over main color loop, 1dc into next dc drawing A through last 2 loops, rep from * to last dc, 1dc into turning ch with A. Turn.
4th row. Using A ch3, skip first dc, 1dc into each dc to end, working over yarn loops on 2 central dc of each block in B and 1 central dc of each block of A, ending with 1dc into turning ch. Turn. These 4 rows form pattern and are repeated throughout. They can also be worked from the chart (see diagram chart).

Two-color diamond jacquard pattern.
This pattern consists of multiples of 6 stitches, plus 1 and a turning chain. Ch21 using A.
1st row. Using A, work 1dc into 4th ch from hook, 1dc into each ch to end. Turn. 19dc.
2nd row. (right side) Using A, ch3, join in B, skip first dc, using

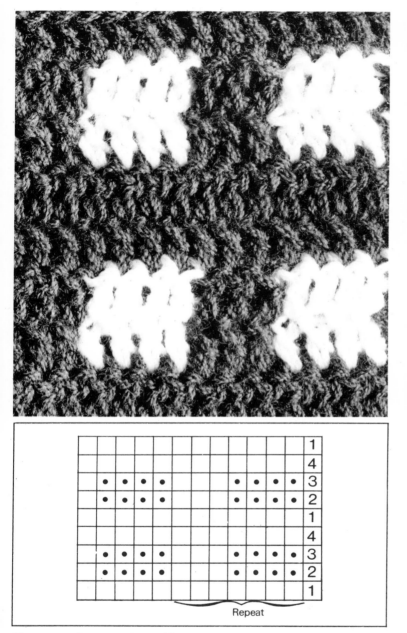

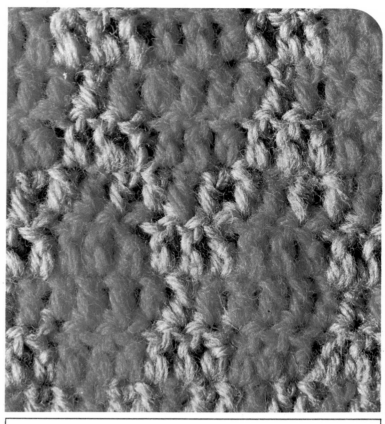

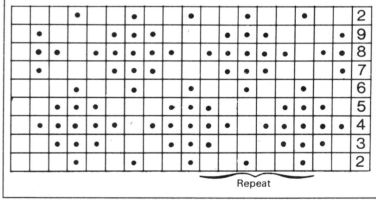

Top: two-color square jacquard pattern
Bottom: chart for the two-color square jacquard pattern

Top: two-color diamond jacquard pattern
Bottom: chart for the two-color diamond jacquard pattern

A work 1dc into next 2dc drawing B through last 2 loops of last dc, *using B work 1dc into next dc drawing A through last 2 loops, using A work 1dc into next 2dc drawing B through last 2 loops of last dc, rep from * to last 4dc, using B work 1dc into next dc drawing A through last 2 loops, using A work 1dc into last 3dc working last dc into turning ch. Turn.

3rd row. (wrong side) Keeping yarn not in use on wrong side, ch3 in A, skip first dc, 1dc into next dc drawing B through last 2 loops, *using B work 1dc into each of next 3dc working over yarn loop on central dc and drawing A through last 2 loops of last dc, using A work 1dc into each of next 3dc working over yarn loop on central dc and drawing B through last 2 loops of last dc, rep from * to last 5dc, using B work 1dc into each of next 3dc working over yarn loop on central dc and drawing A through last 2 loops of last dc, using A work 1dc into last 2dc working last dc into turning ch. Turn.

Continue changing yarns in this way and working over loops on row below, keeping yarn not in use on wrong side of work.

4th row. Ch2 in A, work 3rd ch in B, skip first dc, *using B work 1dc into next 5dc, using A work 1dc into next dc, rep from * to end working last dc into turning ch. Turn.

5th row. As 3rd.

6th row. As 2nd.

7th row. Ch2 in A, work 3rd ch in B, skip first dc, using B work 1dc into next dc, *using A work 1dc into next 3dc using B work 1dc into next 3dc, rep from * to last 5dc, using A work 1dc into next 3dc, using B work 1dc into next dc, using A work 1dc into turning ch. Turn.

8th row. Ch2 in A, work 3rd ch in B, skip first dc, using B work 1dc into next 2dc, * using A work 1dc into next dc, using B work 1dc into next 5dc, rep from * to last 4dc, using A work 1dc, into next dc using B work 1dc into next 2dc, using A work 1dc into turning ch. Turn.

9th row. As 7th.

Rows 2-9 form pattern and are repeated throughout. They can also be worked from the chart (see diagram chart).

627

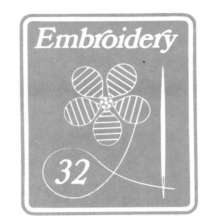

Cross-stitch in fashion

Cross-stitch features in traditional peasant embroideries of many countries, with motifs inspired by insects, flowers, animals and trees. Use these simple cross-stitch designs to give a gay peasant look to dresses, skirts and blouses.

As fashion becomes more and more a matter of achieving individuality, so the scope grows for making your own clothes and adding your own inventive touches.

Embroidery, for example, is the ideal way of personalizing a garment, and cross-stitch, one of the simplest to do, is particularly well suited to dress embroidery.

Provided you use an even-weave fabric, working a design is a simple matter of counting threads and following a chart or pattern. Choose threads according to the fabric—for example, six-strand floss or pearl cotton on linen, crewel wools on lightweight woolen fabrics, silky or metallic textured threads for evening wear. Whether the color scheme is one of toning or contrasting is a matter of personal choice. An interesting color combination to try is a panel embroidered in a shade which contrasts with the main part of the dress.

Scandinavian pattern

This pretty pink and brown design is worked in cross-stitch linked with backstitch to satin stitch blocks. The detail is worked in six-strand floss on a white background.

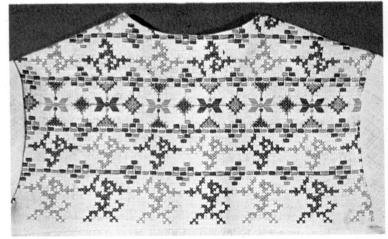

A pretty way to use Scandinavian motifs for dress embroidery

This design would also look attractive worked in one color such as brown on beige, or navy on a pale blue ground.

Moth and flower design

Because of its depth, this unusual border is an ideal design for embroidering the hem of a skirt or a dress. Work it either as a single band or in rows of bands.

The moth motif is sufficiently pretty to be worked on its own, and would look most striking worked in silver or gold thread. The embroidery illustrated is worked in pearl cotton No.8 in pink, gold and green. The fabric is a plain, even-weave linen with 18 threads to one inch.

The design is shown actual size so that the illustration can be used as a working chart.

General rules of dress embroidery

Always work the embroidery on the garment section before making the final article so that you are working on a flat surface and there is a minimum amount of fabric to cope with. Work across seam allowances so that the embroidery goes right into the seamline when the garment is completed.

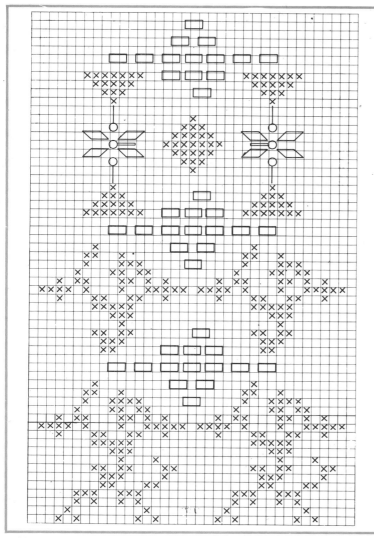

▲ Chart of the Scandinavian design for the yoke of a dress
▼ Moth and flower design, actual size

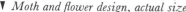

▲ Use the moth motif for a pretty effect on the front panel of a tunic or dress. If the fabric has fewer threads to the inch, the moth will be larger.

Beautiful bolsters to make

Home Sewing 6

Bolsters are special occasion pillows. It doesn't matter if you choose a luxurious Turkish style or a tailored bolster with gathered and buttoned ends, their shapes mix and match easily with any furnishing style.

Suitable fabrics

Any closely woven medium or heavyweight fabric, such as linen, firm tweed or velvet, is suitable for bolsters. Very lightweight or loosely woven fabric like lawn or soft tweed is unsuitable as it will pull at the seams. For bolsters with soft gathered ends choose a supple fabric such as velvet or velours. For maximum impact choose plain fabrics or fabrics with interesting textures and apply decoration in the form of appliqué bands or braiding.

Fabrics with large or one-way patterns may be difficult to match at the seams, so be careful about choosing these.

Fabrics for making the lining should be firm and closely woven. If you choose down and feathers for a filling, use down-proof fabric, whereas muslin or cotton sateen are better choices for Dacron or kapok fillings.

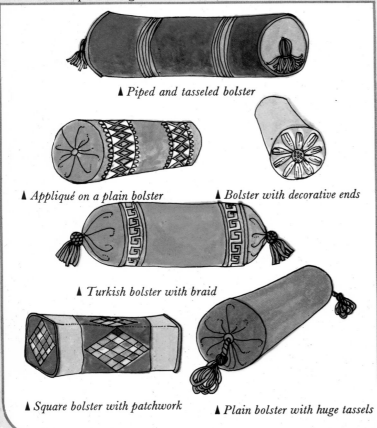

▲ *Piped and tasseled bolster*

▲ *Appliqué on a plain bolster*   ▲ *Bolster with decorative ends*

▲ *Turkish bolster with braid*

▲ *Square bolster with patchwork*   ▲ *Plain bolster with huge tassels*

Turkish bolsters

These are the easiest bolsters to make as the cover simply consists of one piece of fabric seamed down the middle, gathered at both ends and finished with cords or large tassels for decoration.

You will need

For a Turkish bolster about 11 inches in diameter and 34 inches in length:

- ☐ 1yd 36in wide fabric for the cover
- ☐ 1½yds 36in wide fabric for the lining
- ☐ 4½lbs feathers and down or 5lbs kapok or Dacron for filling
- ☐ Matching sewing thread, basting thread
- ☐ 4 large tassels (you can buy them in the notions department or make your own)
- ☐ 1½yds rayon cord, without tassels
- ☐ Scissors
- ☐ Chalk, string, 13in square of brown paper and thumbtack for making a template

The lining

Measure and cut the lining fabric into two pieces, a body piece 1yd square and a piece 18 by 36 inches for the ends.

Fold the yard of lining in half, right sides facing, and baste and stitch two 10 inch long seams as shown in figure **1**, taking ½ inch seam allowance.

Make a circular brown paper template 13 inches in diameter, as follows: Fold paper square into quarters. Attach one end of string

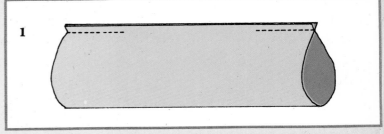

1

to chalk. Hold chalk at top right corner and pull string along the straight edge to top left corner. Fix string at this point with tack. Now, draw with chalk along paper from top right to bottom left corner in an arc. Cut along this line and open out. Then, using the template as a pattern, cut two circles from the remaining fabric. Pin and baste one of the circles to one end of the tube of lining fabric, right sides facing, then stitch the circle into place, taking a 1 inch seam allowance. Snip into the seam allowance of the lining

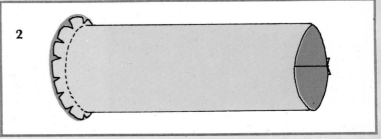

2

tube as shown in figure **2**. Repeat for the other end.

Turn the lining right side out, through the opening, and insert the filling. The filled lining should be fairly firm but squashy.

Close the opening firmly with slip stitch.

The cover

Fold the yard of cover fabric in half, right sides facing, and baste and stitch along the edges as shown in figure **3**, taking a ½ inch seam allowance. Press the seam open.

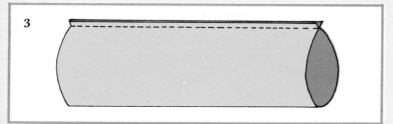

3

Pin, baste and stitch a $\frac{3}{4}$ inch turned hem at each end of the tube, leaving an opening of 1 inch in each hem (figure **4**).

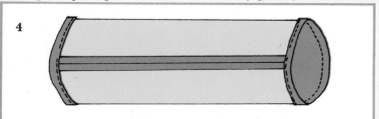

4

Turn the cover right side out.

Cut the length of rayon cord in half and thread one piece through one of the turned hems. Close the 1 inch opening. Gather hem along the cord so that the end is closed and tie the cord decoratively but firmly. Sew a tassel to each end of the cord (figure **5**).

Insert the filled lining into the open end of the cover and finish that end the same way.

5

Fitted bolster with gathered ends

These bolsters are tailored with a zipper opening in the body and neat gathered ends finished off with self-covered buttons.

You will need

For a bolster 7 inches in diameter and 17 inches in length:

☐ $\frac{3}{4}$yd 36in wide fabric for the cover
☐ $\frac{3}{4}$yd 36in wide fabric for the lining
☐ Matching sewing thread, basting thread
☐ Two 1in diameter button molds
☐ 15in zipper to match the cover fabric
☐ $1\frac{1}{2}$lbs down and feathers or 2lbs kapok or Dacron for the filling
☐ Scissors
☐ Chalk, string, 9in square of brown paper and thumbtack for making a template

The lining

From the lining fabric measure and cut a body piece $26\frac{1}{2}$ inches by 19 inches. The remaining fabric is for cutting 4 circles 9 inches in diameter for the ends.

Make a template from the brown paper (use the same method as given for the Turkish bolster), and cut the 4 circles from the lining fabric using this template as a pattern.

Make the lining as for the Turkish bolster.

The cover

Measure and cut out three strips from the cover fabric, one strip $26\frac{1}{2}$ inches long by 19 inches wide for the body, and the other two strips $26\frac{1}{2}$ inches long by 5 inches wide for the ends.

Fold the body piece of the cover fabric in half and pin and baste the edges together taking $\frac{1}{2}$ inch seam allowance. Baste firmly down the full length. Stitch a 2 inch seam at each end (figure **6**). Do not remove the basting, but press the full length of the seam open.

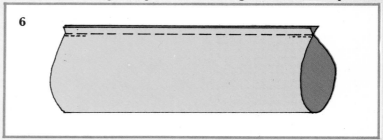

6

Place the closed zipper, right side down, over the basted opening. Baste the zipper firmly into place (figure **7**). Turn the tube right side out and hand sew the zipper into place using a firm backstitch with only a tiny stitch showing on the surface.

Remove the basting and turn the cover to the wrong side.

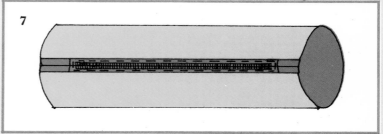

7

Buttoned and gathered ends

Take one of the 5 inch strips of cover fabric and fold in half, right sides facing. Baste and stitch the ends together taking a $\frac{1}{2}$ inch seam allowance. Press the seam open and turn right side out. Place the wrong side of the ring of cover fabric to one of the lining circles. Baste and stitch together (figure **8**) taking a 1 inch seam allowance. Snip the seam allowance on the cover fabric and make a line of gathering stitches around the top edge of the ring as shown. Draw up these gathers firmly and finish off securely. The ring of fabric is now gathered up so that it lies against the lining circle (figure **9**).

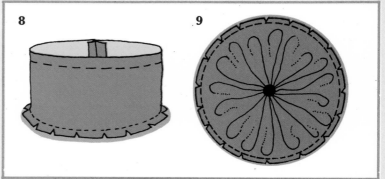

8   **9**

Cover a button mold using remnants of cover fabric and sew the button to the gathered end to cover the center of the gathering. Make the other end of the bolster in the same way.

Baste and stitch the buttoned ends to the body tube, right sides facing, as shown (figure **2**) for the lining of the Turkish bolster.

Turn the cover right side out and insert the filled lining through the opening.

Taking it to the cleaners

Dry cleaning was discovered by a Frenchman named Jean-Baptiste Jolly in 1825, after a maid had accidentally upset a lamp over a tablecloth. Jolly observed that the area which had been soaked with kerosene had dried spotlessly clean. He began to experiment and eventually developed a process which he called "dry cleaning" to distinguish it from the soap and water method that at the time was the only known means of cleaning clothes.

Today, fully automatic cleaning machines and highly refined cleaning fluids are employed in the removal of dirt and stains. You can choose between using a professional dry cleaner, who may offer specialized cleaning services, or if you prefer to do-it-yourself, many laundermats now include dry-cleaning machines on their premises.

Professional dry cleaners handle, literally, tons of clothes and household items everyday, and most of them clean perfectly. The kind of dry-cleaning processes used depends upon the composition of the article being cleaned, but there are some fabrics and fabric finishes which can present problems to a dry cleaner because they will not stand up to the dry-cleaning process. By understanding some of the problems of dry cleaning yourself, and trying to give the dry cleaner all the information he needs about the type of stain and composition of the soiled article, you will find that the results achieved are far more satisfactory.

Will it dry-clean?

Whenever you buy garments which you know will have to be dry-cleaned, check to see if there is a label or hang tag giving dry cleaning instructions. Although garments may appear to be made of fabrics which are recommended for dry cleaning, special finishes may have been applied which present difficulties at different stages of processing. Linings or interfacings may have been added to the garment which are unsuitable for dry cleaning—some interlinings of raincoats, for instance, are composed of rubber impregnated fabrics, or plastic, which either dissolve or harden if immersed in dry-cleaning solvent.

Save labels or hang tags which give details about the finish or the composition of a garment, particularly if it is trimmed with materials such as imitation leather.

Problem fabrics, finishes and accessories

Laminated fabrics and interlinings

Garments made of bonded fabric must be carefully examined before dry cleaning. Although stronger adhesives are now being used which will withstand solvent processes, bonded fabrics manufactured two or three years ago may have included adhesives which will dissolve in the cleaning process.

Raincoats and wind-breakers usually have interlinings which will not withstand the dry cleaning cycle. Your dry cleaner is likely to recommend that these garments should be wet cleaned, providing that the fabric and color will withstand wet processing. Otherwise, it will be necessary to remove the interlining before dry cleaning and replace it after processing.

Animal skins—real and fake

Although dry cleaners accept real suede and leather garments for dry cleaning and the results are entirely satisfactory, some suede-like materials or fabrics with a suede-simulated finish will not clean. Latex or rubber cement has generally been used to fix the pulverized cotton or rayon fibers to the base fabric and this will dissolve in solvent.

Fur-trimmed garments should also be treated with caution.

Occasionally, fur trim is stuck onto a garment, and adhesives which are used for this purpose will dissolve during processing.

Fears about felt

You may find that dry cleaners are pessimistic about dry-cleaning felt garments. Many of them experience difficulties in processing because of the occasional changes made by manufacturers in the fiber content of the fabric. Felts are now being manufactured with mixed fibers in varying proportions, such as 70 per cent wool and 30 per cent rayon. These different fibers are sometimes dyed in different colors, using dyes of varying formulations. Felt also has a tendency to shrink because the fabric is made by a felting process and not woven or spun.

Various kinds of velvet

Velvets can be made of silk, rayon acetate or cotton, and different cleaning processes are applied to the different fibers. Make sure your dry cleaner knows which particular fiber your garment is made of.

If velvet is allowed to become too badly soiled and therefore requires pre-spotting before cleaning, normal spotting methods may not be applicable. To insure satisfactory results, have velvet cleaned frequently before spots and dirt become difficult to treat.

Fancy finishes

Some fabric finishes and printed fabrics can present difficulties at any of the different stages of dry cleaning. Flock prints, for instance, are manufactured by spraying an adhesive onto fabric and then blowing cotton fiber onto the wet adhesive. During dry cleaning, either the adhesive will dissolve in the cleaning fluid or, if the adhesive is of the polyvinyl type, it will become hard and brittle. Flock printed fabrics would be rejected by a dry cleaner as being unsuitable for cleaning.

Fabric finishes which impart a pattern or design to the surface of fabric, such as moiré or ciré satin, can give rise to problems during spotting processes.

Generally, if a garment is likely to receive hard wear and become badly soiled, it is better to avoid those fabrics and finishes which present dry cleaning problems.

Buttons, belts and trims

It is a wise precaution to remove all buttons and buckles before having a garment dry cleaned. Most buttons are fragile, being made of glass, plaster or plastic, and will not stand up to the mechanical action of dry cleaning.

Dry cleaners are sometimes reluctant to accept belts for cleaning, particularly those which are backed with plastic or other synthetic material. Stitched belts made of self fabric are usually acceptable, but if you suspect that the interlining is made of a fabric which will not clean, then dry-clean the belt yourself with a commercial liquid cleaner. This is preferable to risking damage in the professional dry cleaning process.

Decorative effects on garments are sometimes achieved by using sequins, rhinestones, beads or plastic motifs which are cemented onto the fabric with plastic cement. The dry cleaning process can destroy decorations of this kind completely, and you should ask your cleaner's advice about the safety of applied decorations.

Dry cleaning services

A garment should be carefully checked for holes before handing it over for cleaning—a small tear is likely to become a large rent during the mechanical action of dry cleaning.

Some dry cleaners provide a repair and valeting service and will, for a reasonable sum, mend tears and rents.

Does dry cleaning harm garments?

One of the most frequent complaints about dry cleaning is that the process takes the "body" out of fabric, leaving it limp. It is usually suggested that this is because the natural oils have been removed by the solvents and detergents used in dry cleaning. In fact, the lightweight feel of a fabric after dry cleaning is due more to the absence of dirt than the removal of natural oils.

When woolen fabrics are finished, the cloth contains up to one per cent of fatty matter and during wear the cloth picks up grease, together with grit and soil, which adheres to the fatty matter. The general wearing of the fabric is offset by the accumulated weight of dirt and it is not until the garment is cleaned that the real substance of the worn fabric becomes apparent.

To cope with customers' reactions, it has become the practice of dry cleaners to apply retexturing agents after dry cleaning. Various substances have been developed and are used as retexturing agents by the dry cleaning industry, the most popular being paraffin wax. Some cleaners offer retexturing as part of their service, while others make a small extra charge.

Spots and stains

Although you may wish to treat small spots and stains on garments yourself, it is advisable to leave removal of larger stains to a dry cleaner.

Removing stains is a highly skilled process involving a knowledge of fabric, chemicals and the nature and composition of the stains themselves. Usually, dry cleaners prefer customers to send stained garments for treatment as soon as possible after the accident has occured. The stain can be set in the fabric if treatment is delayed and becomes more difficult to remove. Emergency treatment can be applied: water based stains, for instance, can be treated with clean water and greasy stains dusted with talcum powder or powdered chalk. Whatever action is taken, the dry cleaner should be told the nature of the substance which caused the stain and the fluid or chemicals which have been applied as an emergency measure. Successful stain removal depends on quick action. Giving your dry cleaner adequate and accurate information enables him to treat the stain properly without time-consuming tests and experiments.

The jumper conversion

In this chapter, the basic dress pattern, from the Creative Hands Pattern Pack given in Volume 22, is converted into two jumper dresses—a day version, and one for the evening with a wide flared skirt. The day version has front body darts, while on the evening version the front shaping is achieved with slanting bust darts instead of the usual darts.

Full instructions are given for increasing the flare of a skirt to as much as a full circle. Suitable fabrics, the new patterns, and the layouts for both versions are given here so that you will be ready to start sewing by the next chapter.

The secrets of achieving perfect proportioning

Cutting the basic pattern to create new styles is fun and being able to do it shows real progress in dressmaking. At the same time, it is very important to know where to cut the pattern because misplaced seams can spoil a garment.

Decorative seaming, whether vertical, diagonal or horizontal, is very attractive, but all seams must be considered in relation to the length and width of the finished garment.

By careful seaming and proportioning you can create a definite line, such as a square, elongating or flowing line. But if you have a square build, or if you are tall and thin, a similar line will only tend to accentuate it and you will need to alter the proportions to suit you.

Proportioning does not mean that you must have equal lengths of bodice and skirt when the garment is finished. It means that all parts of the garment divided by seams remain in good proportion to each other when the garment is worn, and do not emphasize figure faults or make the garment look clumsy. Nor should the outline of a design be destroyed by bad positioning of seams—they should flatter a figure as well as enhance the style.

Finding the correct position for the horizontal seam

The position of the horizontal seam on the jumper is determined by your figure type, height and size. Consult Dressmaking chapter 3, p. 54, on figure types before you read the following paragraphs.

To find the cutting line for the horizontal seam, first read the instructions for your figure type, then modify them according to your height and size.

Figure type
Standard: 5 inches below the waistline.
Large bust: First consider all the information given in Dressmaking chapter 3, page 54, relating to the particular problems of a large bust, before deciding to make the jumper. The cutting line must be determined very carefully but, unless the bust is very much larger than the hips, the cutting line should be around hip level. This gives emphasis to the widest part of the hips, thus helping to balance the large bust proportions.

Leave plenty of seam allowance on bodice and skirt horizontal seams to allow for adjustments when fitting.

If your bust is much larger than your hips, pin the front and back pattern pieces together along the side and shoulder seams over strips of paper. Slip the pattern over your shoulders and pin. Place a length of dark colored tape around your body over the pattern where you think the cutting line for the horizontal seam should go. Pin the tape down and look at the line from the front and the sides to see if the position is right for you.

Large hips: All figure types with larger hip proportions should cut the pattern around hipbone level, 3 to 4 inches below the waist. This puts the emphasis of width on a narrower part of the body.

Height
Short, 5ft 3in and under: There is no way to create the impression of length through horizontal seaming, but the jumper can look right for you as long as the sections are perfectly proportioned.

Mark the cutting line 3 to 4 inches below the waistline, but when you are cutting out the dress leave at least 2 inches for the horizontal seam on both bodice and skirt so that you can check and perhaps adjust the seam line on the basted garment. This way any adjustments made will not interfere with the length. Here is a guide to the proportioning for short figures.

For a day length jumper, the skirt should look a little shorter than the bodice. For a full length evening jumper, you may be able to drop the horizontal seam line if your hip proportions are good.

Medium to tall, 5ft 4in to 5ft 9in: See instructions under Figure Type where the cutting lines given were for average heights.

Very tall, 5ft 10in and over: Most tall people have to cope with the problem of a long waist or long legs, or both. Since the horizontal seaming divides these lengths, it presents no real problem. However, the following will help you to determine the right position for the seam.

Pin the front and back pattern pieces together along the side and shoulder seams over strips of paper. Slip the pattern over your shoulders and pin it.

Place a length of dark colored tape around your body over the pattern where you think the cutting line for the horizontal seam should go. Pin the tape down and look at the line from the front and the sides to see if the position is right for you.

Size
Small to average: See previous instructions under Figure Type and Height which were based on small to average sizes.

Larger sizes: This problem must be taken into consideration when making the jumper.

If your bust size is over 38 inches, you should use the darts on the pattern and fit the bodice. A loose look will only add to your size. On the other hand, the gentle flare of the skirt on a fitted bodice, combined with a carefully positioned horizontal seam, will create a very flattering line.

Suitable fabrics

Whether for day or evening wear, choose a fabric that is suitable for the style of the dress you are making. Fabrics with horizontal, vertical or diagonal design details are not suitable as the design would interfere with the cut of the jumper—especially the day dress with its topstitching detail.

Fabrics to suit the geometrical appearance of the day length jumper are:

☐ Firmly woven tweed and worsted woolens.
☐ Double knit wool, polyester and heavy cotton jerseys.

Fabrics to suit the soft look of the evening jumper are:

☐ Wool, silk and rayon crepes.
☐ Lightweight wool and polyester jerseys.
☐ Pure silk and rayon satins.

Yardages

Day length jumper: The following yardages are for the given pattern length. If you want to make the skirt longer, don't forget to add the extra skirt length required on each pattern section to the yardage.

54 inch width, without one way—sizes $32\frac{1}{2}$ and 34, $1\frac{3}{4}$ yards; size 36, $1\frac{7}{8}$ yards; size 38, 2 yards; sizes 40 and 42, $2\frac{1}{4}$ yards.

54 inch width, with one way—sizes $32\frac{1}{2}$ and 34, $1\frac{3}{4}$ yards; size 36, $1\frac{7}{8}$ yards; size 38, $2\frac{1}{8}$ yards; sizes 40 and 42, $2\frac{1}{4}$ yards.

36 inch width, without one way—size $32\frac{1}{2}$, $2\frac{7}{8}$ yards; size 34, 3 yards; size 36, $3\frac{3}{8}$ yards; sizes 38, 40 and 42, $3\frac{1}{2}$ yards.

36 inch width, with one way—size $32\frac{1}{2}$, $3\frac{1}{8}$ yards; size 34, $3\frac{1}{4}$ yards; size 36, $3\frac{1}{2}$ yards; size 38, $3\frac{5}{8}$ yards; sizes 40 and 42, $3\frac{3}{4}$ yards.

Evening jumper: The following yardages are for a dress length of 58 inches. If you want to make the skirt longer, don't forget to add the extra skirt length on each pattern section to the yardage.

54 inch width, without one way—sizes $32\frac{1}{2}$ and 34, $2\frac{7}{8}$ yards; size 36, $3\frac{1}{4}$ yards; size 38, $3\frac{3}{8}$ yards; size 40, $3\frac{5}{8}$ yards; size 42, $3\frac{3}{4}$ yards.

54 inch width, with one way—size $32\frac{1}{2}$, $3\frac{3}{8}$ yards; sizes 34, 36 and 38, $3\frac{1}{2}$ yards; sizes 40 and 42, $3\frac{3}{4}$ yards.

36 inch width, without one way—size $32\frac{1}{2}$, $4\frac{3}{4}$ yards; size 34, $4\frac{7}{8}$ yards; size 36, $5\frac{1}{2}$ yards; size 38, $5\frac{5}{8}$ yards; sizes 40 and 42, 6 yards.

36 inch width, with one way—size $32\frac{1}{2}$, $6\frac{1}{2}$ yards; size 34, $6\frac{5}{8}$ yards; sizes 36 and 38, $6\frac{3}{4}$ yards; size 40, $6\frac{7}{8}$ yards; size 42, 7 yards.

By careful proportioning and seaming, jumper-style dresses can suit all figure types ►

Making the new pattern

First, make sure you have plenty of paper handy for copying the pattern so that you will not have to cut up the original.

Copy and cut out the front and back of the basic dress pattern (pieces 1 and 2 in the Pattern Pack given in Volume 22).

Next, mark your waistline on the new pattern. To determine its position, use either the corrected bodice muslin pattern (see Dressmaking chapter 17, page 336) or use a measuring tape.

Front: Square neckline

Mark out the new neckline (figure **1**).

Measure 2 inches along the shoulder seam from the neck edge and mark. Measure 5 inches down, make another mark and connect to the center front edge by a straight line, using a tailor's square or set square. Measure back along this line 3½ to 4 inches, depending on how wide you want the neckline to be, and mark. Connect this point to the original mark on the shoulder seam.

Cut out the new neckline as shown in red.

Back: Neckline

Mark off the same distance from the neck edge along the back shoulder seam as you did for the front. Then, measure 1¼ inches from the neck down the center back line and connect both marks with a curved line (figure **2**).

Cut out the new back neck curve.

Center back seam

If you want to make the jumper fitted, it is necessary to curve the center back seam slightly before you start dividing the pattern for the bodice and skirt.

Draw a gentle curve (figure **2**) through the waist from a point about 4 inches below the waistline to a point about halfway between the waistline and neck. Make sure that the curve tapers gradually back into the original line.

If you are also using the back darts, you must compensate for the center back curve by drawing the darts a little less deep, or the back will become too fitted.

Any further adjustments necessary to make the jumper more fitted should be left until the fitting stage.

Cut out the center back curve.

Horizontal seam

Measure your correct horizontal cutting line at equal distances below the waistline across both back and front pattern pieces and draw in the new lines.

Measure the side seams of the bodice to make sure that they are the same length on the back and the front. Also check that the skirt back side seam is the same length as the skirt front side seam.

Since the back and front skirt patterns are very much alike, mark the pieces clearly

636

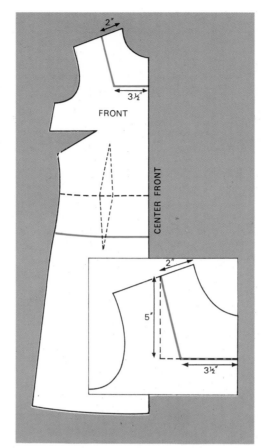

1. ▲ *Making the square neckline on the front*
2. ▼ *Making the new back neckline on the Back and curving the Center back seam*

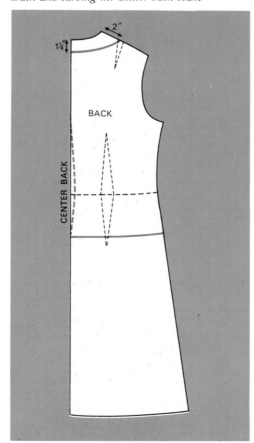

front and back and mark in the center front and center back before cutting along the horizontal lines.

Also mark the center front line on the bodice as "fold," since there is no seam in the bodice front.

Cut the pattern along the horizontal lines.

Back and front facings

Here is a new type of facing to finish the neck and armhole edges of the dress.

To avoid the bulky finish which two separately cut facings would make over the shoulders, the neck and armhole facings are cut in one piece.

Lay the center back and front of the bodice pattern pieces along the straight edge of a sheet of paper and draw around the top edges (figures **3** and **4**). Remove the patterns and draw in the inside lines of the facings as shown.

Reduce the width of the facings a little over the shoulders as shown by the red dash lines (figures **5** and **6**). This insures a perfect finish when the facings are stitched in place and avoids showing a roll along the edges. Cut out the facing patterns.

The skirt darts

If you are not fitting the dress with body darts, use the skirt pattern as it is, ignoring the darts. But if you are stitching body darts, you must deal with the darts in the skirt before cutting out the dress. Here are two ways to do this.

Method A. Leave the darts in the skirt in line with the body darts so that they look like one long dart after stitching.

Method B. Alter the shape of the skirt pattern (figure **7**). This method will also add a little more flare around the hem.

To achieve this, first fold the darts on the pattern pieces to meet along the stitching lines and hold them securely in position on both sides of the pattern with transparent tape. Lay the center of each skirt pattern piece along the straight edge of a piece of paper, wider than the pattern, and pin along the center line.

Slash each pattern from the hem upward to the end of the dart. Spread the slash until the pattern lies flat and pin down. Draw around the new pattern shape, remove the original and cut out the new skirt pattern. Transfer back and front markings.

Increasing the skirt fullness

The diagram (figure **8**) shows you how to add width to the skirt and obtain the lovely fullness shown in the evening version of the jumper. The short skirt can also be made with an increased flare.

Using this method you can even increase the skirt until it is a quarter circle, for a circular skirt, but you would need to increase the number of slashes to get a good waist curve.

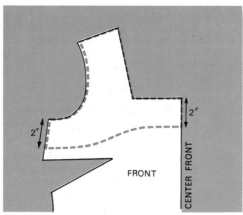

3. ▲ *Making the front neck and armhole facing*
4. ▼ *Fold off dart and then make back facing*

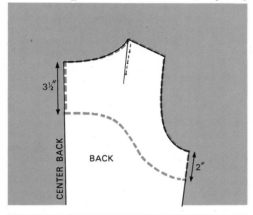

5. ▲ *Reducing the shoulder width of front facing*
6. ▼ *Reducing the shoulder width of back facing*

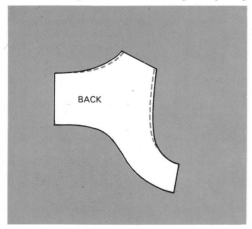

Step A. First prepare the back and front skirt patterns as shown in figure 7, then make two more slashes evenly spaced between the slash for the darts and the side seam. Make all three slashes to within ⅛ inch of the waistline, which means cutting through the darts.

Step B. Pin the center of each skirt pattern piece to the straight edge of a sheet of paper large enough to accommodate the extra width and length needed for the evening skirt.

Step C. Following figure 8, add 24 inches to the width of the hem of the short skirt by spreading each slash 2 inches along the hem line. Pin the pattern down.

You will notice that the waistline starts to curve up and lift considerably toward the side seam. This is correct to retain the waist measurement.

Step D. Draw around the pattern edges with a pencil and extend the side seam. Plot out the new hemline, an equal distance from the original, using a yardstick, and draw in the new curve. Cut out the new skirt pattern.

**Making the pattern
for a slanted side bust dart**

For the soft molded look of the evening dress, the front body darts are dispensed with and the side bust darts are slanted.

The slanting of the side bust dart should be about 45 degrees. Although this may vary from person to person it should not be more than 45 degrees. If you alter the dart by that amount, you can always lessen the slant without much trouble if it is too steep for you. This will be done at the fitting.

To make the new pattern, pin the front bodice pattern to the straight edge of a sheet of paper wider than the pattern. Draw around the pattern and into the dart. Remove the pattern.

Extend the upper side seam (figure 9) downward as shown. Then turn the end of the dart upper stitching line downward through 45 degrees, make a mark on the extended side seam and connect the point of the dart to it.

To find the lower stitching line, measure the distance between the original dart stitching lines at the side seam and mark off this distance between the new stitching line and the side seam. Draw in the dart lower stitching line from side seam to point.

Draw a straight line from the dart point through the center of the new dart to meet the new side seam and then connect it to the dart lower stitching line at the original side seam, as shown.

Cut out the new pattern but do not cut out the dart yet, as it may not be in the correct position.

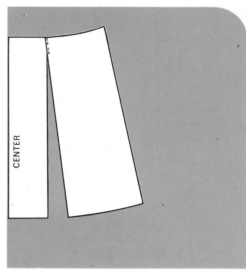

7. ▲ *Folding off the dart on the skirt pattern*

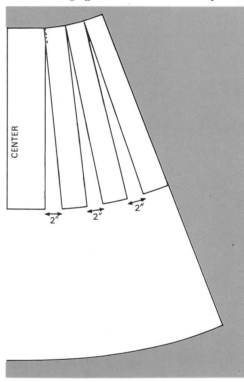

8. ▲ *Lengthening skirt and increasing the flare*
9. ▼ *Altering the slant of the side bust dart*

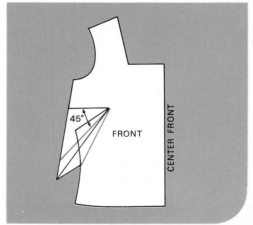

Day length jumper

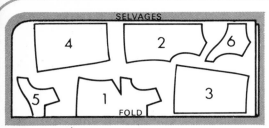

▲ *54 inch width, with & without one way, sizes 32½ & 34*

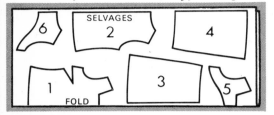

▲ *54 inch width, without one way, sizes 36 & 38*

Layouts for the jumpers

The layouts given here are for the day length jumper without extra flare, and the evening jumper. If you increase the flare on the skirt, you may need extra yardage. Using these layouts as a guide, first make a trial layout on paper before buying the fabric to calculate how much extra you need.

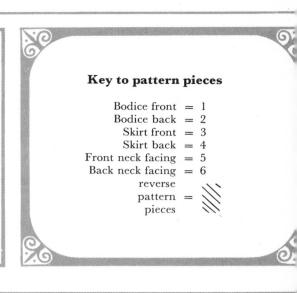

Key to pattern pieces

Bodice front = 1
Bodice back = 2
Skirt front = 3
Skirt back = 4
Front neck facing = 5
Back neck facing = 6
reverse pattern pieces = ///

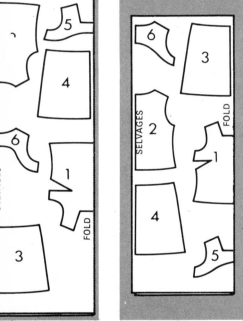

▲ *54 inch width, without one way, sizes 40 & 42*

▲ *54 inch width, with one way, sizes 36 & 38*

▼ *54 inch width, with one way, sizes 40 & 42*

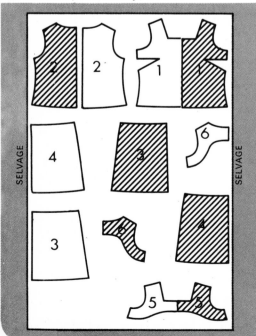

▼ *36 inch width, without one way, sizes 32½ & 34*

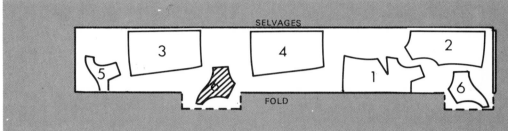

▼ *36 inch width, without one way, sizes 36 & 38*

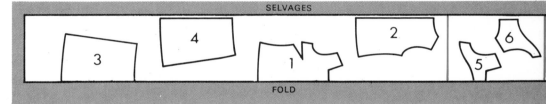

▼ *36 inch width, without one way, sizes 40 & 42*

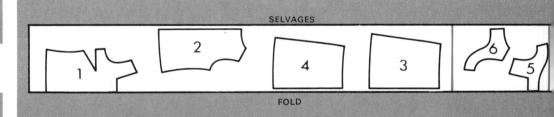

▼ *36 inch width, with one way, sizes 32½ & 34*

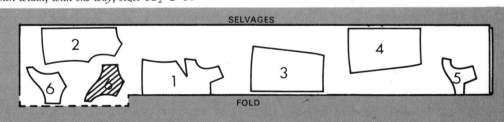

▼ *36 inch width, with one way, sizes 36 & 38. Alternative layout for section between red lines on layouts for fabrics without one way, sizes 36 & 38*

▼ *36 inch width, with one way, sizes 40 & Alternative layout for section between red lines on layo for fabrics without one way, sizes 40 & 42*

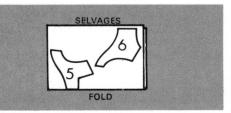

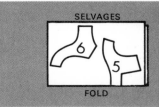

638

Evening jumper

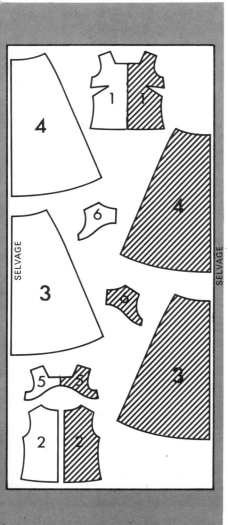

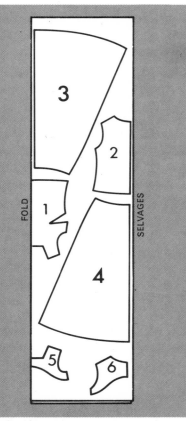

▲ *54 inch width, without one way, sizes 32½ & 34*

▼ *54 inch width, with one way, sizes 32½ & 34*

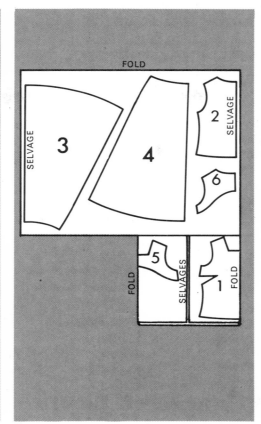

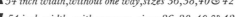

▲ *54 inch width, without one way, sizes 36, 38, 40 & 42*

▼ *54 inch width, with one way, sizes 36, 38, 40 & 42*

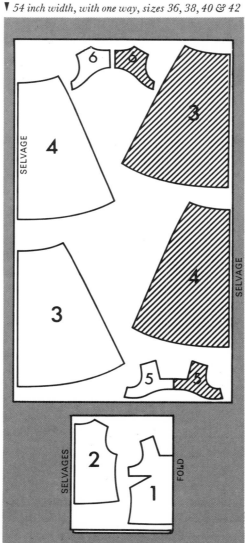

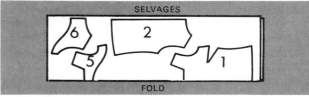

▲ *36 inch width, without one way, skirt layout for all sizes*

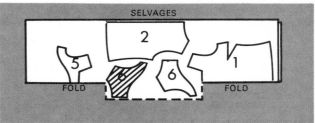

▲ *36 inch width, without one way, bodice layout sizes 32½ & 34*

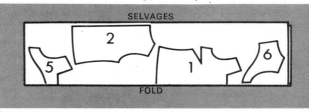

▲ *36 inch width, without one way, bodice layout sizes 36 & 38*

▼ *36 inch width, without one way, bodice layout sizes 40 & 42*

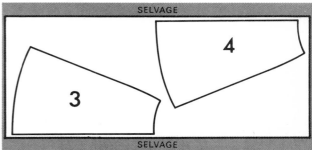

▼ *36 inch width, with one way, skirt layout for all sizes*

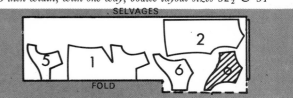

▼ *36 inch width, with one way, bodice layout sizes 32½ & 34*

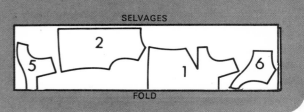

▼ *36 inch width, with one way, bodice layout sizes 36, 38, 40 & 42*

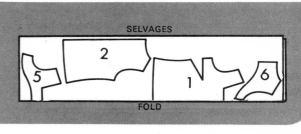

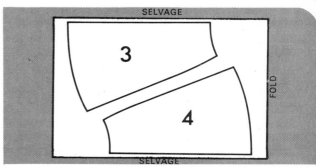

639

Fashion Flair

Shawls to suit

Take a suit, make a matching stole, add a fringe, and you're right in fashion. Here are the instructions for a simple-to-make stole and poncho that will add variety to your wardrobe.

Don't forget that directions for easy-to-do fringe were given on pages 26 and 52.

Creative Hints. Triangular stoles are easy to make. Take at least a 45in square of fabric (36in fabric is too narrow) and fold it into a triangle.

Make a stole which goes with more than one dress: Use two triangles of different fabrics and make the stole reversible. Make the fringe in two matching colors alternating them along the edge.

Stoles are hard to keep in place, so make sure that the lining fabric isn't slippery.

To make a pattern for a shaped poncho, cut a 45in square of paper. (You can stick newspaper together to make up the required size.) Fold the square into a triangle, cut across the diagonal and discard one of the triangles. Mark a 10in neckline in the center along the diagonal and shape the sides and bottom edges as shown in sketch No.1. Fold the triangle in half to check that the shaping is regular on each side. Open up and cut out the pattern.

Using the pattern cut out two pieces of fabric, sew the shoulder seams and make a button opening on the left shoulder. Finish off the neck and lower edges and add a fringe to the hem.

1. *Evening poncho in soft silk or crepe with fine silky fringe.*

2. *Triangular tweed shawl to match a suit or dress with heavy contrasting fringe.*

3. *Fine crochet or lacy-knit triangular wrap dipping at the front and finished with tassels.*

4. *A heavy brocade shawl made to match an evening skirt.*

Pattern Library

Floral scroll design

This enchanting shadow work design is embroidered entirely in white on pink, giving a delicate, fragile effect. Texture and detail have been added by working parts of the design in long and short stitch, outline stitch and masses of tiny satin stitch spots.

This type of design would be charming as a centerpiece on a dainty tea cloth or for glamorous curtains in nylon organdy. Place the design repeats to suit the finished article. Shadow work is made in double backstitch and is best worked with one or two threads of 6-strand floss.

Bow belles

Until you are experienced in two-color knitting, the simplest way of adding interest and color to knitted fabrics is by applying stitches directly onto the finished fabric. Used carefully, the contrasting threads will add to the effect of the background stitch and look as if they had been knitted as part of the fabric. The silver belt illustrated shows a pretty way of using woven bows.

Applying additional colors
The three different effects illustrated here are all simple to work. The silver belt with woven bows could also be worked using the contrasting cluster stitch, or you could use the very effective imitation smocking to make cuffs on a baby's dress.

Woven bows
The bows or groups of gaily colored straight stitches are threaded through one central stitch which gives them a "knitted in" look. Use them to brighten any stockinette stitch pullover or cardigan, either by working them as a border or all over the fabric. The same motif using only one contrasting color has been used for the belt.

Cluster stitch
These chunky bobbles or clusters of yarn can be worked while the knitting is in progress or after completion, by threading the yarn several times around a group of two or more stitches. The groups of clusters are just as effective when worked in the main color and can be used on

642

either the purl or knit side of stockinette stitch. To work them in as part of the fabric, work to the position where a cluster is required, slip the next 3 stitches onto a cable or spare needle, pass the yarn around these stitches from back to front until the cluster is the desired size (6 or 8 times should be sufficient), then work the 3 stitches from the holder in the usual way and continue to the position for the next cluster. Where a very chunky effect is required, work 2 rows on the 3 stitches before winding the yarn around.

Mock smocking
There are many variations of smocking which can be used to give a distinctive touch to adults' or childrens' garments. Just as with cluster stitches, the stitches which are to represent the smocking can be worked as the knitting is in progress or can be added after the knitting is completed. Unless a very tight, close effect is desired, ribs which consist of more purl or background stitches than knit stitches show the smocking to its best advantage. For example, use a P3, K1 rib, P4, K1 rib or, for a larger repeat P5, K2 rib, taking alternate sections of the knitted rib stitches together with contrasting thread as given for cluster stitches, but only winding the yarn around once or twice. The illustration used here shows a traveling rib, which gives a diamond effect. The contrasting yarn has been applied after the fabric has been completed at the points where the diamonds join.

▲ *Woven bows in different colors on stockinette stitch give a butterfly effect*

▲ *Cluster stitches can be worked in the main color or in contrasting yarn*
▼ *Mock smocking with contrasting stitches worked over a traveling rib stitch*

▲ *A simple yet effective knitted belt with woven bows worked to match the color of the dress*

Silver belt with woven bows

Size

To fit 26-28in waist. For every additional inch required, add 6 sts to the total given.

> ### Gauge
> 6 sts and 8 rows to 1 in over stockinette stitch worked on No.5 needles.

Materials

Bucilla Spotlight
One ball main color A
One ball of contrast color B
One pair No.5 needles
(or Canadian No.8)
Four small curtain rings
Waist length of lining fabric
3in wide satin or taffeta
Waist length of stiffening
2½in wide

Belt

Using No.5 needles and A, cast on 151 sts.
Beg with a K row, work 21 rows st st.
Place marker thread around central st to mark center back of belt. Bind off.

Woven bows

Thread a length of B into a darning needle. Work from marked center st outward to ends.
With RS facing, insert needle from WS through center of 3rd st to the right of central st and 1 row below bound-off edge. Pass yarn under center st 5 rows below bound-off edge and insert needle from front to back of work in center of st 3sts to the left of center st and 1 row below bound-off edge. Bring needle from back to front 1 row below last st to right of central st and pass through center st, then insert needle into center of st below last st to left of central st taking the needle through to the back. Continue in this way until 7 threads have been passed through the central st. Begin the next group of threads by bringing the needle from back to front of work 1 row below bottom left-hand corner of last st of previous group and work 1 group to the left of first group. Continue in this way to left-hand edge of belt, then work right-hand to correspond.

Finishing

Cut stiffening to same size as belt. Cut lining, allowing ½in extra seams all around. Tack stiffening to belt and cover with lining, turning in edges and sewing securely around all edges. Cover 4 rings with B (see Crochet Know-how chapter 7, page 126), and st to belt ends so that half the ring shows on RS.
Using A, make tie cords by crocheting a ch or by tying ends of 3 strands of yarn tog. Thread cords through rings for front fastening.

High-necked and handsome

This elegant, high-buttoned, open-work crocheted cardigan has been cleverly designed in a range of sizes suitable for all figure types. Made in beige or in your favorite color, it looks stunning with skirts and pants.

Sizes

Directions are for 34in bust. The figures in brackets [ ] refer to the 36, 38, 40, 42 and 44in sizes respectively. Length down center back, 21½[21½:22:23½:24]in. Sleeve seam, 16½[17:17:17½:17½:18]in, adjustable.

Gauge
For 34, 36 and 38in sizes, 1 motif of 3dc and 1 picot measures approximately ¾in worked on No.E crochet hook.
For 40, 42 and 44in sizes, 1 motif of 3dc and 1 picot measures approximately 1in worked on No.F crochet hook.

Materials
3-ply fingering yarn 9[9:10:10:11:11] 1oz balls
One No.E (3.50 mm) crochet hook for 34, 36 and 38in sizes
One No.F (4.00 mm) crochet hook for 40, 42 and 44in sizes
Seven buttons

Back

Using No.E[E:E:F:F:F] hook, ch87[91:95:87:91:95].
1st row (WS) Into 6th ch from hook work 1sc, *ch3, 1sc into first of 3ch to form 1 picot, 1sc into next ch, ch2,
644

skip 2ch, 1sc into next ch, rep from * to end of row. Turn.
2nd row Ch3, 2dc into ch2 sp of previous row, *ch2, 3dc into next ch2 sp, rep from * to end of row. Turn.
3rd row Ch4, *work 1sc, 1 picot, 1sc all into next ch2 sp, ch2, rep from * ending with 1sc after 2nd last dc of previous row. Turn.
The 2nd and 3rd rows form patt and are rep throughout.
Continue without shaping until work measures 14 [14:14:15:15:15]in from beg, ending with a 2nd row.

Shape armholes
1st row 1ss into each of next 2 sts, 2sc into next sp skipping picot, patt to last sp, 2sc into sp skipping picot. Turn.
2nd row 1ss into next st, work 1sc, 1hdc, 1dc all into next sp, patt to last sp, work 1dc, 1hdc, 1sc into last sp. Turn.
3rd row As 1st.
4th row 1ss into next st, ch3, 2dc into next sp, patt to last sp, 3dc into last sp. Turn.
Continue without shaping until armholes measure 7[7:7½:8:8:8½]in from beg.

Shape shoulders
Keeping patt correct, work 2 patt less at each end of next and following alt row. Work 1 row in patt.
Work 1[1:1½:1:1:1½] patt less on next row.
Fasten off.

Left front

Using No.E[E:E:F:F:F] hook, ch47[51:59:47:51:59].
Work as given for back until

left front measures same as back to armhole, ending with a 2nd patt row.

Shape armhole
Work ½ patt less at armhole edge on next 6 rows.
Continue without shaping until armhole measures 5[5:5½:6:6:6½]in from beg.

Shape neck
Keeping patt correct, work 1 patt less at neck edge 2[3:3:2:3:3] times, then ½ patt less 1[1:2:1:1:2] times.
Continue without shaping until armhole measures same as back to shoulder, ending at armhole edge.

Shape shoulder
Work 2 patt less at shoulder edge of next and following alt row. Work 1 row. Work 1[1:1½:1:1:1½] patt less on next row. Fasten off.

Right front

Work as given for left front, reversing all shaping.

Sleeves

Using No.E[E:E:F:F:F] hook, ch35[39:39:35:39:39].
Work in patt as given for back, inc one dc at each end of 6th and every following 2nd row, working the dc into patt as they are made, until there are 4 complete motifs extra at each end.
Continue without shaping until sleeve measures 16½ [17:17:17½:17½:18]in from beg, or desired length to underarm.

Shape cap
Work ½ patt less at each end of every row 13[14:14:13:14:14] times. Fasten off.

Finishing

DO NOT PRESS.
Leave each piece flat between damp towels until dry. Join shoulder, side and sleeve seams. Sew in sleeves.
Front borders. Using No. E[E:E:F:F:F] hook, work 1 row sc up right front, around neck and down left front, working 3sc into front corner sts. Turn.
Work 3 more rows sc in same way.
5th row (buttonhole row) Mark positions for 7 buttons on left front, the first one 8 sts from the lower edge and the 7th one in the neckband with 5 more spaced evenly between. Work in sc to end, making buttonholes as markers are reached by working ch3 and skipping 3sc. Work 3sc into corner sts and dec 7sc evenly around neck edge, work in sc to end. Turn.
6th row Work in sc to end, working 3sc into each ch3 sp of previous row. Turn.
Work 3 more rows sc, dec 7 times evenly around neck edge on 3rd row.
Last row Work 1 row sc, continuing along lower edge of cardigan. Fasten off.
Sleeve edges. Work 1 row sc along cuff edge of each sleeve. Fasten off.
Sew on buttons to correspond to buttonholes.

▼ *Stitch detail*　　　*Casually elegant coordinated with a skirt* ▶

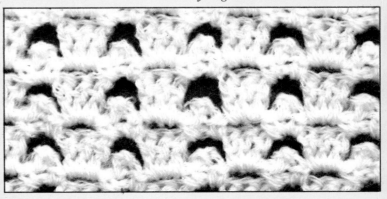

Jacquard patterns from charts

Crochet Know-how 33

Whether working jacquard patterns in two colors or more, the method is the same as that given in chapter 32, page 622. Since jacquard patterns produce a thick fabric, it is better to limit the colors used to three when working garments.

Base your designs for jacquard crochet on geometric shapes or simple designs—cross-stitch embroidery patterns can be used as a guide for motifs. Don't attempt anything too complicated because the depth of crochet stitches will not allow very fine detail.

Copy the design you have chosen onto squared graph paper calculating one stitch for each square. Leave the stitches to be worked in the main color as an empty square and mark the stitches to be worked in a contrasting color as a black dot in a square. If you wish to use a third color in the design, mark these stitches as a crossed square. Work the design in single or double crochet, remembering that single crochet will give a closer overall pattern, whereas double stitches are fairly long and will distort a rounded shape.

When changing from one color to another, be sure to draw through the last loops of the last stitch with the yarn of the next color. Always keep the yarns not in use at the back of the work. Also, when working over a group of stitches, remember to work over the loop of yarn on the row below. This prevents overlong loops at the back of the work and makes it easier to keep an even gauge.

The white cottage motif shows how a simple design can be converted into a chart and worked in crochet. Designs such as this could be worked for pockets or as motifs for pillows.

You can use up remnants of yarn while practicing the three jacquard patterns on these pages, trying out color variations of the patterns. If test squares of crochet are worked to the same size, they can be joined together to make a colorful afghan.

▲ *Three-color geometric jacquard pattern*
▼ *Chart for three-color geometric jacquard pattern*

▼ *Two-color triangle jacquard pattern*

▼ *Chart for two-color triangle jacquard pattern*

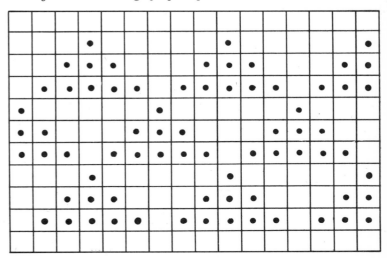

▲ *Two-color checked jacquard pattern*

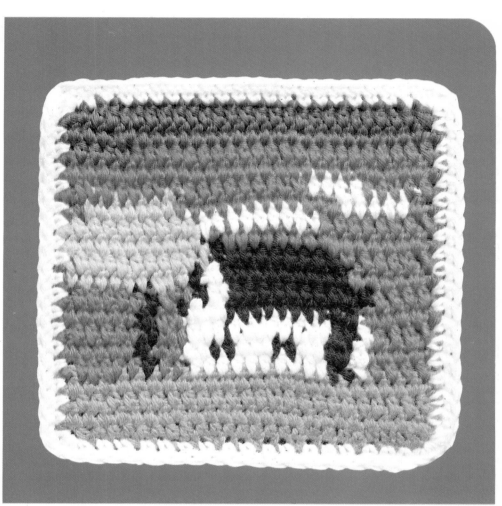

▲ *A simple picture worked in crochet from a chart. Using six colors, the motif produces a thick fabric suitable for a mat or potholder.*

▼ *Chart for two-color checked pattern*

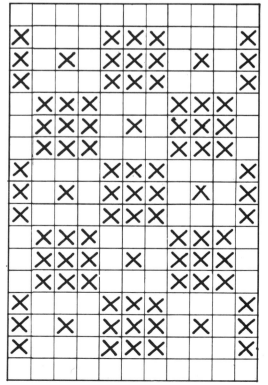

▼ *Chart for cottage motif*

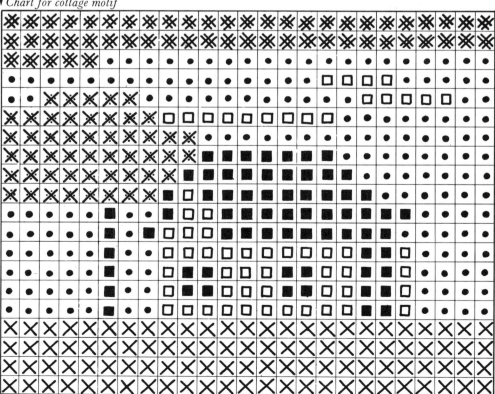

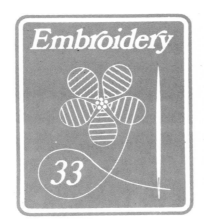

Stitch and shadow

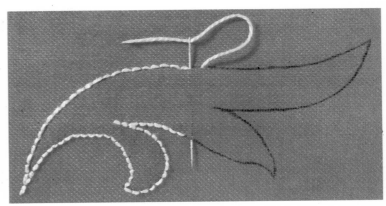

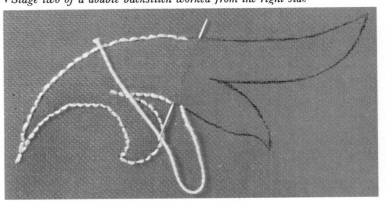

▲ *Stage one of working a double backstitch from the right side of work*
▼ *Stage two of a double backstitch worked from the right side*

This delicate form of embroidery is of oriental origin and is traditionally worked entirely in white threads on a white, semi-transparent fabric. Because of its delicate nature, it is best to use it on articles which receive little use. The stitch characteristic of shadow work is double backstitch, the long stitches crossing at the back of the work to create the opaque shadow effect.

Preparing a design

When preparing designs for shadow work, either use a transfer or the tracing method described in Embroidery chapter 4, page 68. Designs can be transferred to either the wrong side or the right side of the fabric, depending on whether you choose to work the design from the back or the front of the work.

Unless the work is to be held taut when completed, such as a lampshade, shapes which require a stitch deeper than $\frac{3}{8}$ inch should be worked in sections. This is because the stitches at the back of the work are inclined to snag if they are long and loose. The flower motif illustrated is an ideal shadow work design and would be effective worked as a border on a curtain or as a single motif on a dainty apron. The petals are worked in two sections.

Fabrics to choose

Transparent or very fine fabrics are essential for this type of embroidery because the filling stitches must show through. Several types are suitable—organdy, fine linen lawn, cotton/Dacron lawn and nylon chiffon.

Selecting colors and threads

The beauty of shadow work is in the effect of embroidery showing through fabric. It is far more effective to work thread in one color on a matching or strongly contrasting background fabric—for example, navy on white, or dark blue on pale blue—than to use a variety of different colored threads.

Fine threads are recommended, particularly six-strand floss.

Working the embroidery

The stitch used in shadow work is called double backstitch or herringbone. The crossed threads lie at the back of the work so that they show through the transparent fabric and the backstitches lie on the surface as an outline. Double backstitch can be worked from the right or wrong side of the work (see illustrations) and this is a matter of personal preference. However, if other stitches are being used on the surface for detail, you will find it more convenient to work from the right side so that you can observe your progress and not constantly have to turn the work over. An embroidery frame is advisable to prevent the stitches from pulling and causing puckering. When working around a curve, the backstitches on the inside of the curve must be smaller than on the outside curve (see illustra-

tion). Always keep stitches perpendicular to their base.
N.B. The stitches in the illustrations above are worked on a large scale for clarity only.

Varying the theme

Shadow work designs can be worked entirely in double backstitch, but, as with most forms of embroidery, the introduction of other stitches adds interest. Outline stitch, chain stitch and backstitch, plus their variations, are particularly effective used with shadow work. Satin stitch, French knots and eyelet holes add dimension as well as texture to a design.

Drawn threadwork and shadow work make a delightful combination—so do appliqué and shadow work. Shapes are applied to the back of the work and pin stitched.

Plain edges

There are several methods of edging shadow work articles.

Hemstitching A plain hemstitched hem looks crisp and neat. Because the fabric is transparent, make the hem double so that the raw edge does not show through.

Buttonhole stitch This gives a strong edging. To give additional strength to the edge of fine fabrics, turn under a very narrow hem, baste and work the buttonhole stitching over the hem.

Decorative edges

Picots These can be made at regular intervals along a buttonhole-stitched edge by working them at the same time as the edging.

Twist the thread several times around the needle and insert the needle back into the last buttonhole stitch. Continue the buttonhole edging.

Loop picots Make a small loop over a pin. When the loop is secured by the following stitches, remove the pin and continue.

Buttonhole ring picots Take the thread back along the buttonhole stitches just worked to form a semi-circular loop and cover with buttonhole stitches. Continue working the buttonhole edging.

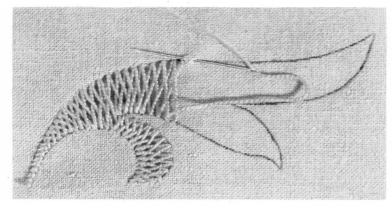

▲ *Stage one of working a double backstitch from the wrong side of work*   ▲ *Stage two of a double backstitch worked from the wrong side*

▼ *Working a picot edging*   ▼ *A simple flower motif for you to copy. Trace the design from this illustration.*

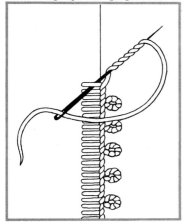

▼ *Working loop picots*

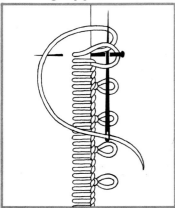

▼ *Working buttonhole ring picots*

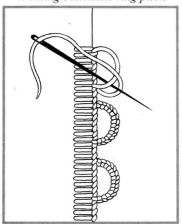

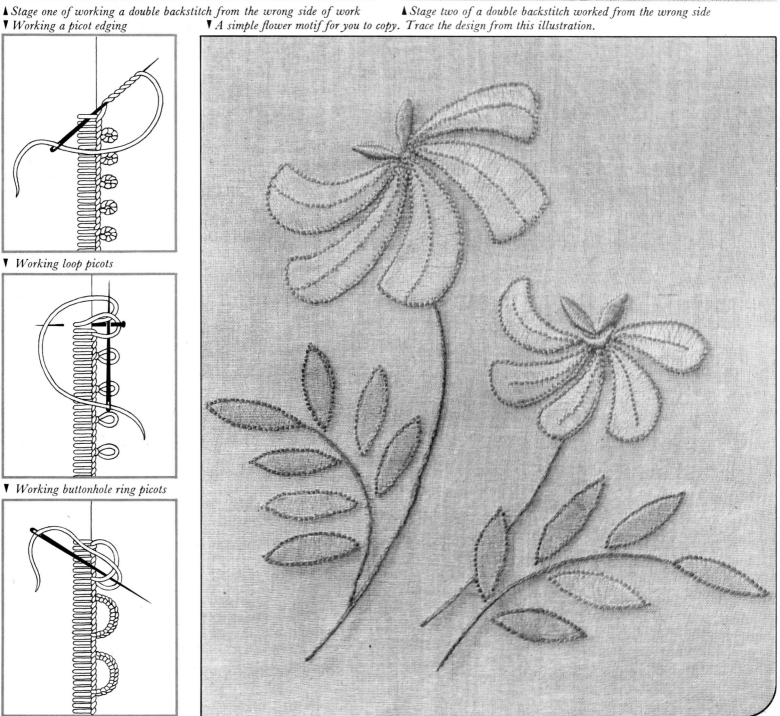

Be your own valet

Clothes need cherishing. Once that meant valets and ladies' maids for the rich—hard work for the rest. Now new fabrics and cleaning aids make it easier to keep clothes looking good.

The secret is good organization, for which there are three golden rules:
1. Take a few minutes every day to put clothes away properly and in good order.
2. Deal with problems quickly—the sooner done, the easier to correct.
3. Set aside time periodically for a session of cleaning and repairing.

1. Day-to-day

To get maximum wear out of clothes, especially suits, wear them in rotation. (Never wear a suit more than two days running.) Always hang clothes up immediately after wearing—if left in a warm heap, wrinkles will set.

For day-to-day care you need a first-rate clothes brush, also a sponge or plastic foam "brush" to deal with surface dust. Brush outdoor clothes before you hang them up (dust is grit and grit eventually breaks up the fibers). Close all fastenings as you hang up the garments to help support them. Then give them a while to air before consigning them to the closet.

Put each garment away in the state you would like to find it the next time you go to put it on. Try to find a special place to hang clothes which are unfit to wear so that you can see at a glance how much of your wardrobe is wearable.

Collars. Clean greasy collars or necklines marked with make-up with a grease solvent. Frequent, light sessions do a much better job than intermittent scrubs.

Removing fluff. If your regular clothes brush or sponge won't do the trick, wind a piece of transparent tape around your hand, sticky side out, and rub gently over the surface of the cloth. (This works wonders with velvet.)

Hangers. Good hangers are essential. Coats and suits should hang on shaped wooden hangers. For dresses, pad thin hangers with old stockings and cover with fabric. Hang skirts by the carrier loops inside the waist: longer skirts need a center loop to prevent them from sagging. Long dresses with waistlines should be folded over and hung from the waist. Never hang garments from bare wire hangers.

Closets. Try not to squash too many clothes into too small a closet—try to keep out-of-season clothes in bags on a rod in the attic or spare room.

2. Deal with problems fast

Deal with tears, loose buttons, unstitched hems and stains as soon as possible. (For stain removal, see Take Care chapter 5, page 614). Here are a few other pointers.

Buttons. Buttons are not always well-sewn on ready-made clothes. Sew them on properly before they unravel and drop off.

Cigarette burns. Good clothes should always be mended by a professional mender, but you can use the following method to patch up unimportant, lightweight clothes. But practice on a scrap first! Snip away all charred threads with scissors, leaving a neat, clean round hole. Cut out a patch of matching cloth slightly larger than the hole, and another patch of fine polythene sheeting (dry cleaners' bags will do) the same size. Place the damaged cloth on a sheet of clean paper, right side down. Place the polythene patch over the hole, and then the cloth patch. Press the area gently with a hot iron until the polythene melts and glues the two fabrics together invisibly. This trick is not suitable for heavier fabrics.

Hems. If desperate, use transparent or double sided tape to hold up a small length of hem until you can resew it.

Knitwear, pilling and matting. It's worth investing in a special knitwear "defuzzer." Stroke lightly, and always in one direction.

Pulls and catches. If the thread is not broken, ease it back into the weave as far as possible, then hook the remaining loop through to the wrong side with the head of a pin.

Rips and tears. Again, these should be repaired by a professional mender or carefully darned. As a last resort, adhesive fabric tape can be stuck to the wrong side of the torn cloth. It will stand up to washing but not dry cleaning.

3. The periodic session

Suits. In between dry cleanings, sponge and press about every six weeks. To do this, you need a stout, wooden-backed brush, a pad of fabric to hold under the shoulder seams, a couple of damp cloths —and a firm hand.

First brush the suit vigorously. Lay it flat and rub all over with the dampened cloth to remove loose surface dust. Carefully lay the area to be pressed on the ironing board, cover with a clean damp pressing cloth and press firmly, lifting the iron gently each time. Take care! If the suiting is a blend, too hot an iron and too much pressure can ruin the cloth.

Pressing pants. See Take Care 4, p. 598.

Pressing jackets. To press a jacket, it's worth making a pressing pad—a 9 inch square bag stuffed firmly with kapok. Start by pressing the collar, opened out and flat. Next, using a damp pressing cloth, press the right front, working from the hem to the waist. As you work, move the pressed area away from you so that it will not become creased again. Now press the area above the waist (for a woman's jacket, use the pressing pad to press the bust). Press underarm area. Press back. Press left underarm. Press left front. Next, sleeves. Sleeves must never have a crease, and the simplest way to avoid this, if you do not have a sleeveboard, is to lay the edge of the sleeve so that it falls over the edge of the board and therefore does not receive the weight of the iron. Turn the sleeve gradually so that the whole area is pressed. Finish the shoulders by pressing over the pad to keep the curve full. Finish by opening the lapels out flat and pressing from the underside. Don't fold the collar or lapels back and press—just roll them gently back into position.

Shine. Shine can only be removed temporarily since it usually means the cloth has worn thin. Before attempting any remedial action, brush the suit thoroughly, then sponge the worn area with a solution of vinegar and warm water. Rinse with a clean cloth wrung out in warm water. Pass a hot iron very lightly over a damp cloth on both sides of the shiny area—to "swell" the fibers, not to flatten them! For light materials use the same system, but add ammonia to water (1 tablespoonful to 1 pint).

Baggy skirts, pants and elbows. You may be able to shrink the cloth back to its original shape. To do this, lay the affected area on the ironing board and cover with a well dampened cloth. Stroke the cloth with the iron without pressing, to force the steam into the fibers. Leave to "set" and dry before further handling.

Pants and pleat creases. For a crisp crease, rub the inside of where it should be with hard household soap. Then press in the normal way with a damp cloth, making sure the crease is in exactly the right position.

Perspiration. If the garment is washable, soak in cool detergent solution (test for colorfastness first). To try to revive color, sponge with a weak solution of vinegar or ammonia before washing (again, test first). Sponge clothes (except rayon) which can't be washed with methylated spirits and rub gently in a circular motion with a dry cloth. To remove odor, first soak the garment in warm water with borax (1 teaspoonful to 1 pint). Wash in warm soapy water to which a few drops

of ammonia have been added. Rinse well. If the fabric is suitable, try to dry in sunshine—sun always has a sweetening effect.

Linings. A cheap, unlined skirt always looks better if it has a lining. Choose a firm, inexpensive rayon fabric.

Knitwear, stretched collars and cuffs. If careful washing and flat drying can't remedy this, darn two or three rows of elastic thread around on the wrong side of the garment.

Metallic embroidery and lamé. To clean gold work or other metallic embroidery, brush gently with bicarbonate of soda. After a few minutes, brush out with a soft, clean cloth.

Artificial flowers. These revive if held in the steam from a boiling kettle.

Feathers. Shake several times in soapy lather. Rinse well in warm, then cold, water, and dry slowly in a warm oven with the door open, taking them out from time to time to curl them over the edge of a blunt knife.

Care of clothes brushes. To get fluff out of a bristle clothes brush, rub warm, dry oatmeal flakes into the bristles and leave for a few hours. Shake, comb out, and rub with a clean cloth. (Too much washing makes bristles soft.) Nylon brushes can of course be washed.

Storage

As mentioned under day-to-day care, it's useless to overhaul a dress and press it beautifully—and then plunge it into an overcrowded closet. Be sure that there is adequate space—do not cram in more clothes than the closet can accommodate. It is best to store out-of-season clothes in plastic bags hung in a dry part of the house. Always have clothes cleaned before storage. Separate heavy and lightweight clothes in the closet. Store knitwear in a drawer, not on hangers; allow air to circulate rather than keeping sweaters, etc, in bags. Always store metallic embroidery and lamé in acid-free paper.

Work basket

A well stocked work basket is invaluable. It should include small supplies of the following: elastic (sufficient for a pair of panties), dressmaker's pins, needles, thread, darning equipment, assorted safety pins, transparent tape, shirt and other buttons, adhesive fabric tape, foam pad, and spot removal fluid—with ammonia, vinegar and borax near at hand, plus clean cloths and a pressing pad.

Patching up color for fashion

Machine-made patchwork brings exciting possibilities—areas of patchwork can be made very quickly and turned into purses, skirts and fashionable garments of all kinds. This method is suitable for patches of 1½ inches and over in length. Remember, patch measurements are always worked out from the length of the sides, not the overall length. A 1½ inch diamond-shaped patch is one where each side measures 1½ inches.

Suitable fabrics

There is a wide range of fabrics available which you can use, such as cotton, fine wool, silk, velvet, corduroy and tweed, but avoid choosing fabrics which are very tightly woven for stitching patches with acute angles, such as diamonds, because the machine needle has to go through several layers of fabric. On the other hand, vinyl-coated fabric, leather and suede work well, because although they are dense fabrics they do not require turnings.

Suitable machines

The sewing machine should be a model with a zigzag stitch for this kind of patchwork. It is possible to sew patchwork with a straight-stitch machine by opening out the pressed seams of the patches and stitching them together along the creases, but the zigzag method is easier and more accurate.

Needles, threads and stitches

Use a No.14 machine needle (continental No.90) and change to a new needle more often than you would usually, as patchwork papers tend to blunt the point. Stitch with a fine thread, No.50 or 60, and use a mercerized cotton or synthetic thread according to the type of material you have chosen.

Choose a thread color that is suitable for the colors in the patchwork. A white thread looks attractive on mixed colors, or you could match the thread to one of the basic colors in the fabric. To maintain an even effect, it is important to use the same color and type of thread throughout the work.

On swing needle machines the "swing" of the stitch (that is, the stitch width) can be adjusted in the same way as the stitch length. As a general guide for machine patchwork, select a swing of 1½ to 2 and a medium stitch length. Loosen the top tension a little.

It will be necessary to adjust the controls slightly according to the fabric and length of the patch. For instance, a 3 inch hexagon will need the stitches to be set further apart than a 2 inch hexagon, although the swing will remain the same.

For the best results experiment with your machine, trying out the stitches on folded scraps of fabric.

Sewing the patches together

Prepare the patches as for hand sewing (see Patchwork chapter 1, page 332). If the finished patchwork is for fashion appliqué, use bonded fiber fabric instead of papers.

Place two patches together with the right sides facing. Make sure that they match evenly, but allow the underneath patch to show just a fraction along the working edge (figure **1**). This way you will be able to see that the stitches are penetrating both patches.

A swing needle swings from left to right and back again. Left is the starting point and you must always start with the needle ready to swing to the left. Turn the balance wheel by hand to discover which way the needle is going to swing and set it ready to swing to the left.

Place the patches under the machine needle and turn the balance wheel toward you so that the needle pierces the top right-hand corner of the pair of patches (figure **2**). Lower the presser foot and stitch, not too quickly at first.

At the left-hand swing the needle should pierce the fabric and papers of the two patches and at the right-hand swing the needle should pass just beyond the side of the patches (figure **3**).

When you come to the end of the working edge, make sure that the needle swings to the right for the last stitch—you will then be ready to swing back to the starting point when you begin the next seam. Give the balance wheel a half turn toward you, lift the presser foot and draw out the patch, leaving at least two inches of thread before cutting off. This is essential as the ends must be tied off to secure the stitching. It is best to use a double knot for this, as it prevents the threads from becoming tangled (figure **4**).

If you prefer, instead of tying off each pair of patches separately, you can stitch a whole series of pairs of patches together in sequence so long as you leave enough thread between them for tying off. The threads are cut afterward.

When stitching diamond patches, it may be necessary with some fabrics to "help" the machine over the points, as there can be up to eight layers of material to penetrate.

Open out each seam and you will see that the patches are joined together with firm, even stitches—straight at the front and criss-crossed at the back (figure **5**).

Add as many patches as you need, keeping the grain of the material running as straight as possible.

When the work is large enough, take out the basting threads and remove the papers. (This will also make it easier to work should the patchwork become cumbersome.) The papers may have been caught by the needle but will pull away easily, and often can be used again.

Finishing

Pressing Machine patchwork should be pressed well, with a steam iron and a pressing cloth. If there is velvet in the patchwork, use a needleboard. Press as if it were hand-sewn patchwork (see Patchwork chapter 1, page 332) and pay particular attention to the edges of the piece if the patchwork is for fashion appliqué.

Lining Although patchwork is a strong fabric if properly stitched and tied off, it is easily distorted because the grain of the fabric used in the patches does not always run in the same direction. Because of this it is necessary to line patchwork that is to be used in large pieces for making garments. The lining fabric then acts as a strengthening base and will take the strain instead of the patchwork.

To line patchwork, place it on the lining fabric, wrong sides facing, and catch the two together at regular intervals (every two patches or so) with tiny stitches. Baste around the edges and then treat the lined patchwork as if it were a single layer of fabric.

Mounting If you have used bonded fiber fabric instead of papers, leave it inside the patches. Catch the bonded fiber fabric to the patchwork at intervals and mount the patchwork on the garment by sewing around the edges with tiny hemming stitches.

If the area of appliquéd patchwork is large, catch it to the fabric of the garment occasionally.

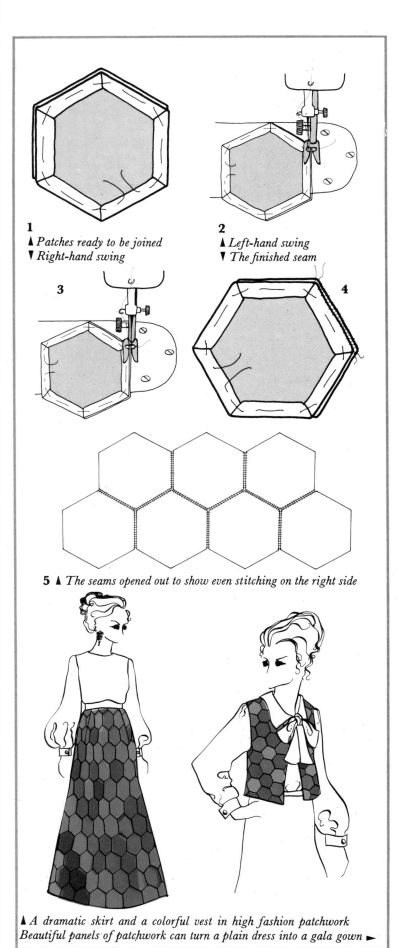

1
▲ *Patches ready to be joined*
▼ *Right-hand swing*

2
▲ *Left-hand swing*
▼ *The finished seam*

3

4

5 ▲ *The seams opened out to show even stitching on the right side*

▲ *A dramatic skirt and a colorful vest in high fashion patchwork*
Beautiful panels of patchwork can turn a plain dress into a gala gown ▶

Embroidery on tulle 2

Closed filling stitches

Once the pattern outlines have been embroidered onto the tulle, the next stage is to work the decorative filling stitches. This chapter explains how to do the most decorative and the most frequently used of this group of stitches. They serve two purposes—first, to cover a large area of tulle with solid filling as quickly and simply as possible and secondly, to look attractive over the large area.

Darning stitch
This is a very quick and easy way to fill in large areas. Work backward and forward, passing the yarn alternately over and under the meshes until the area is complete. Always work two rows of thread in the same meshes so that the return rows fill in the gaps left by the first rows. You can work this stitch in any direction.

Linen stitch
This is another quick way of filling in large areas. Simply work rows of running stitch, diagonally or vertically, and then cross them with horizontal rows of running stitch.

Wavy stitch
Turn the tulle so that the hexagons are vertical.
Work this stitch diagonally taking one thread of the tulle above and one below, skipping a hole in between and picking up one thread with each stitch. Subsequent rows are worked by picking up the threads skipped on the previous row. Leaving more threads between the stitches makes a less wavy line.

Double wavy stitch
With the hexagons horizontal, work a horizontal row of stitches as for wavy stitch, from right to left. Complete the row from left to right by working over the same threads, but picking up the threads left by the first stage of the row to make a crossed stitch.

Staggered running stitch
Work running stitch with a double thread, staggering the stitches by moving one thread along on each row, giving the effect of rows of parallel diagonal lines.

Compound stitch
With the hexagons horizontal, work two rows of staggered horizontal wavy stitch. Then work one row of oblique stitches, sloping in alternate directions, each covering one mesh of tulle. Work each oblique stitch twice over to give double thickness of thread.

Diamond border
Combinations of stitches can make very pretty borders. The one illustrated here, for example, consists of a row of diamonds worked in staggered running stitch. On each side of these diamonds is another row of diamonds worked in cording.

654

▲ *Darning stitch*

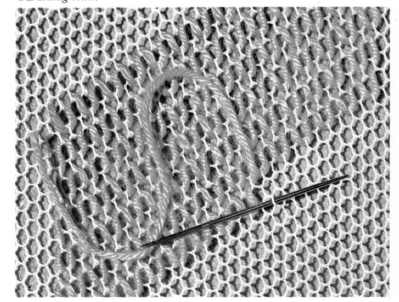

▲ *Wavy stitch*   ▼ *Staggered running stitch*

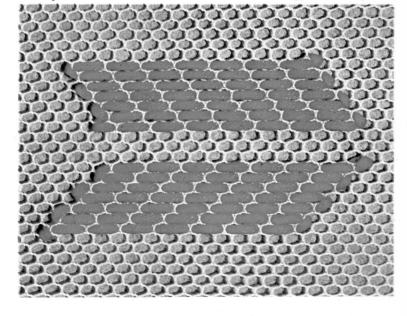

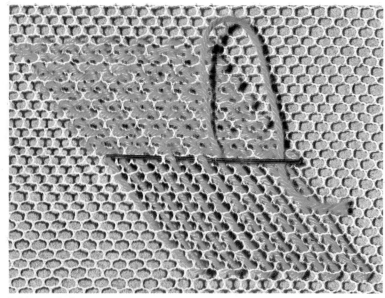

▲ *Linen stitch*

▲ *A pretty christening robe*　　　▼ *Diamond border*

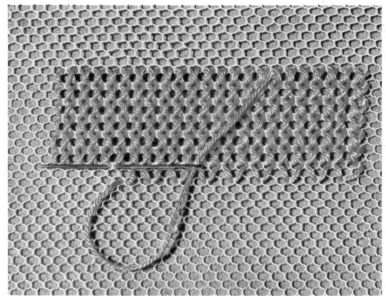

▲ *Double wavy stitch*　　　▼ *Compound stitch*

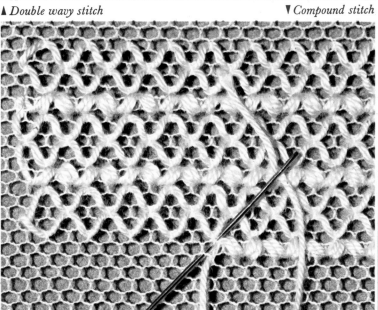

Jumpers easy and elegant

The two elegant jumper dresses from the last chapter are cut out and completed here. Separate sets of instructions are given for the day length jumper—both with and without flare—and for the evening dress. Follow the construction steps in the order given for the quickest, most successful results when making these dresses.

Notions

First make sure you have all the notions necessary. For all the jumpers you will need:

- ☐ 24 inch zipper
- ☐ 1 or 2 spools of buttonhole twist and thicker machine needles for topstitching
- ☐ Hook fastener
- ☐ If you are lining the dress you will need suitable lining fabric ¼ yard less than the dress yardage for fabric without one way
- ☐ If you are increasing the flare on the skirt you will also need ½ yard soft interfacing suitable for the fabric you are using

Day length jumper

These instructions are for the day length jumper without extra flare on the skirt.

Procedure

Here is an outline of the steps in making the jumper:

- ☐ Cutting out
- ☐ Marking
- ☐ Assembling and basting
- ☐ Fitting
- ☐ Stitching the bodice
- ☐ The lining
- ☐ The facings
- ☐ The pocket flaps
- ☐ Making the skirt
- ☐ Topstitching
- ☐ Finishing: zipper, lining, hem

Cutting out

Lay the patterns on the fabric using the appropriate layout for your size and fabric width from Dressmaking chapter 32, page 634. For topstitching the center front seam in the skirt and the horizontal seam, you will need extra-deep seam allowances. The topstitching can vary between ¼ and ½ inch from the seam, so decide on the width and add an extra ½ inch to give you the correct width for these seam allowances.

For all other seams allow ¾ inch, and 2½ inches for the hem.

Marking the pattern detail

For those who now feel confident working with paper patterns, it may no longer be necessary to tailor's tack in a continuous line around all the pattern pieces. Select strategic points only, such as where seams meet, or important shapes, or special seam distances for detail (figure **1**) and make just enough continuous tailor's tacks to guide you, so that you can follow the continuation of the seams without difficulty.

Drawing lines with chalk is another quick way to mark details on fabric, but these lines can be lost very easily when handling the work. You would then have to refer back to the pattern, which could result in inaccurate copying, and you may even have to start ripping. A little extra work at the beginning is worth the effort.

Assembling and basting

Pin and baste the darts, side seams and shoulder seams of the bodice, leaving the center back open. Press lightly.

Pin and baste the skirt seams and press lightly.

Pin the bodice and skirt along the horizontal seamline, carefully matching centers and side seams: Pin and baste, then press this seam into the bodice.

Fitting

If you want to wear the jumper over blouses and sweaters, wear one during the fitting or you may fit the dress too tightly.

Pay special attention to the armholes, since a thick sweater will need extra room. If you have to increase the size of the armholes all around, remember that if you want to wear the jumper on its own, a large armhole can look very ugly. So try on the dress both ways and reach a compromise.

Make sure the horizontal seamline is straight and at the same level back and front.

If the seam is not level, adjust in the following way:

As long as the general hang of the dress is good, just lift or lower the seamline as required, remembering that you must let out from one side of the seam what you take in from the other, otherwise you will upset the hang of the dress.

If the hang of the dress is wrong, go through all the fitting stages of the basic dress in Dressmaking chapter 10, page 196. Finally, check the horizontal seam and adjust as above if necessary.

Correct all the faults, then baste the garment together again for a final fitting.

Stitching the bodice

Stitch all the darts. Then press the body and shoulder darts toward the center. The shoulder darts must lie flat, so if the fabric is thick, make an open dart by slashing along the center toward the point as far as the scissors will allow, and press open. If the fabric frays, just slash the dart past the shoulder seamline and press the rest of the dart flat.

Press the side bust darts flat or open.

Stitch the bodice side seams and press.

If you have fitted the dress closely to the body, you will notice that the curve of the side seam through the waistline has deepened. This makes it difficult for the seam allowance to lie flat after pressing and, as you turn the garment to the outside, you will see that the side seam is strained at the top and bottom.

To enable the seam allowance to follow the contours of the seam, snip into the deepest part of the curve to within ¼ inch of the stitching (figure **2**).

To stop the points of the snipped seam allowance from curling, round them off (figure **3**), then overcast them carefully to prevent fraying which would weaken the seam at this point.

Overcast all stitched seam edges.

Do not stitch the shoulder seams yet.

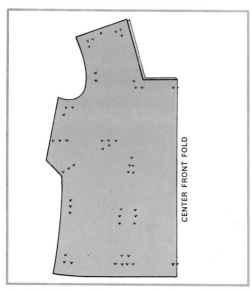

1. ▲ *Tailor's tacking strategic points only*
2. ▼ *Snipping the bodice side seam at the waist*

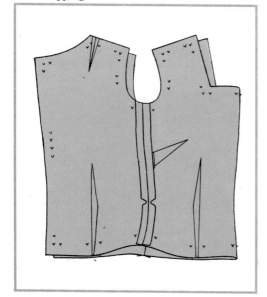

The evening dress has soft, clinging lines ▶
3. ▼ *The snip at the waist, curved and overcast*

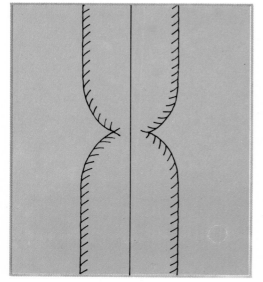

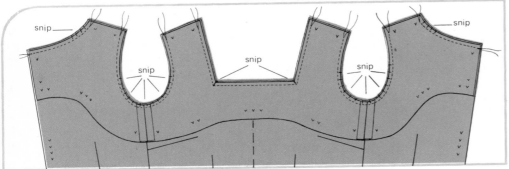

4. *The all-in-one facing stitched in place around the neck and armholes*

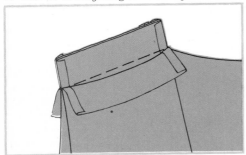

5. *The shoulder seam stitched with facing open*

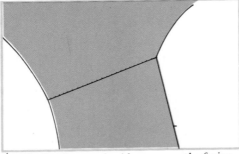

6. *The hand-sewn shoulder seam on the facing*

The lining

If you are lining the dress, it is time to make the lining for the bodice.

Cut out the lining as for the dress, but without facings.

Stitch the darts and seams as for the dress, leaving the shoulder seams open. Press and finish the seams.

Pin and baste the lining to the bodice, with wrong sides facing. See that the raw neck and armhole edges are even and that centers and seams coincide.

The lining seams should face the wrong side of the dress, and dress and lining fabric are used as one when the facings are attached.

The facings

Stitch the facings together in the side seams, leaving the shoulder seams unstitched. Press the side seams open and overcast the lower raw edge.

With right sides facing, pin and baste the facing to the dress, matching seams and centers carefully.

Stitch the facing to the dress (figure **4**) around the neckline and armholes. At the shoulders, stop stitching at the point where the stitching line meets the shoulder seam, as shown. Fasten off the threads securely. Do not stitch the shoulder seams yet.

Trim and snip the seam allowance where shown and turn the facing to the inside. Baste along all stitched edges and press.

With right sides facing, pin and baste the shoulder seams of the dress only (figure **5**), paying special attention to the ends of each seam. These must coincide absolutely or you will have a step where one side

projects when the seams are finished.

Stitch and press the shoulder seams open and work the allowance under the facing. Trim the shoulder seam allowance on the facing to $\frac{3}{8}$ inch and fold it under, so that the edges almost meet over the dress shoulder seam (figure **6**).

Slip stitch them together by hand and press.

The pocket flaps

To break the length of the horizontal seam, you may like to make pocket flaps as shown in the day length version of the jumper. These are entirely optional and only serve to decorate, so you need not apply tailoring techniques.

To make a pocket flap, cut a strip of fabric from the remnants $5\frac{1}{2}$ inches long by 4 inches wide. Fold it lengthwise, right sides facing, and stitch $\frac{1}{4}$ inch seams across both ends (figure **7**).

Turn to the right side, edge baste and press. Topstitch around the outside edges to match the topstitching you will be making on the dress.

Pin and baste the flaps to the horizontal bodice seamline, $2\frac{3}{4}$ inches to each side of the center front line, taking only $\frac{1}{2}$ inch seam allowance on the flaps (figure **8**).

Making the skirt

Stitch the skirt seams, remembering to leave the opening for the zipper in the center back. Press seams open and finish them.

Pin, baste and stitch the skirt to the bodice along the horizontal seamline, matching centers and side seams. If you are lining the dress don't catch the lining into the seam. Press the seam open.

Topstitching

Measure out the distance of the topstitching from the seamline along the horizontal and center front seams (figure **9**).

Then, using buttonhole twist, start topstitching the horizontal seam on the skirt from the right center back to the center front. Pivot the work on the needle when you have reached the corner of the "T" shape at the front, and continue stitching down the center front seam toward the hem.

Topstitch the left side of the skirt, but this time start stitching from the hem, to the left of the center front seam.

To topstitch the bodice, work from the left side of the center back toward the right side. Where the fabric is especially thick, such as over the seam allowance of the pocket flaps, pause before you stitch over the extra thickness and ease the pressure foot onto the work.

Finishing: zipper, lining and hem

The unlined dress. Insert the zipper into the center back opening, starting $\frac{1}{2}$ inch down from the neck edge and using the method that is given in Dressmaking Chapter 7, page 136.

To finish the neck edge, fold under the raw edge of the facing and place the fold over the zipper tape, but leave it clear of the teeth. Hand sew it firmly to the tape and press. Stitch a hook fastener and work a bar on the neck edge to hold it together. Finish all raw edges and make the hem.

7. *The pocket flap folded and stitched*

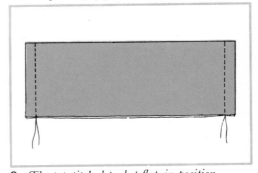

8. *The topstitched pocket flap in position*

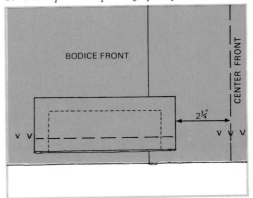

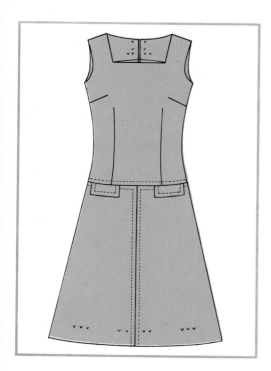

9. *The topstitching lines on skirt and bodice*

The lined dress. Before you insert the zipper, cut the lining along the neck edge just inside the stitching so that the seam allowance on the center back opening and facing can be folded back free of the lining. Insert the zipper, leaving the lining free. Start the zipper ½ inch down from the neck edge and use the method given in Dressmaking Chapter 7, page 136.

Make the skirt lining as for the top skirt, but without topstitching. Join it to the bodice lining along the horizontal seamline and press both seam allowances toward the bodice.

Finish the raw edges and make the hem on both dress and lining.

Fold the center back seam allowance on the lining over the zipper tape and sew it down by hand. Then fold under the raw edge of the facing and place the fold over the zipper tape, clear of the teeth. Hand sew it firmly to the tape and press. Stitch a hook fastener and work a bar on the neck edge to hold it together.

Both versions. Give the dress a final pressing and, when pressing the topstitching, lay it over a double blanket to preserve the roundness of the stitches made in buttonhole twist, taking care that the edge of the seam allowance does not leave an impression on the outside of the fabric.

Day length jumper with extra flare

This is worked like the jumper without extra flare except for the topstitching.

Because of the increased flare on the skirt the top edge is very curved and when the horizontal seam has been pressed open the skirt horizontal seam allowance falls short of the skirt width (figure **10**). To enable the seam to lie flat, the seam allowance will have to be snipped and therefore becomes unsuitable for topstitching. If you did topstitch it, the snips would show up as dents on the outside.

There are two ways to topstitch this seam.

Method A. After stitching the horizontal seam, press the seam allowance on the skirt and bodice together toward the bodice. Trim the bodice seam allowance to ⅛ inch less than the width of the topstitching. Baste the seam allowances together to the bodice and just work the topstitching on the bodice.

Method B. Topstitch the skirt before sewing the horizontal seam and underlay the topstitching with strips of soft interfacing cut on the bias.

Decide on the width of the topstitching and measure this distance from the horizontal seam on the skirt. Mark with pins on the right side.

Using the soft interfacing, cut two bias strips a little less than double the width of the topstitching, and the length of the topstitching along the horizontal seam from the center front to the center back. Do not join them.

Center the strips over the pin line on the inside of the skirt from the center back to center front and position the ends

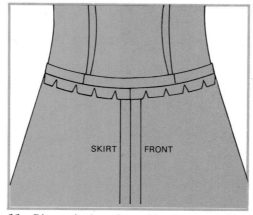

10. *The snipped horizontal seam on the skirt*

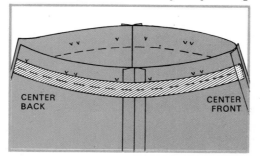

11. *Bias strip basted on skirt for topstitching*

just under the seam allowance on the center front to avoid a dent in the stitching line at this point (figure **11**). If the jumper fabric is thick, you should cut each bias strip at the side seams and slip the ends under the side seam allowances.

Baste each strip to the pin line. Then, using the buttonhole twist, topstitch the skirt over the basting line, starting from the right center back to the center front. Pivot the work on the needle when you have reached the corner of the "T" shape at the front, and continue the stitching down the center front seam toward the hem.

Topstitch the left side of the skirt, but this time start stitching from the hem to the left of the center front seam.

Join the skirt and top. Trim the horizontal seam allowance on the skirt to ½ inch, snip into the seam allowance on the skirt until it lies flat and press (figure **10**).

Finish the raw seam edges and lightly stitch the seam allowance on the skirt to the underlay of the topstitching.

Topstitch on the bodice as for the day length jumper without extra flare.

The evening dress

The jumper is ideal for evening wear. With its clever cut and subtle fit, it will be a firm favorite and a very easy dress to wear.

To achieve the right look—which is soft, long, and molds to the figure—use one of the fabrics recommended in Dressmaking chapter 32, page 634.

When using soft fabrics, especially jersey, use as little darting as possible. Slant the side bust darts as shown in Dressmaking chapter 32, and take any surplus fabric into the side seams and the center back seam. This way you will avoid having to use body darts in the front and the back. Also flare the skirt as shown in the previous chapter.

When marking the pattern details, mark the stitching lines of the new dart on the fabric through small slits made through the pattern.

When fitting you can easily alter the slope of the dart if it is wrong—remember to mark any necessary changes to the dart on the pattern for future use.

Making and topstitching

Follow the same construction procedure as for the day length jumper without extra flare, remembering to press the slanting side bust darts open and to omit the body darts.

Also, if you wish to topstitch the skirt, follow the topstitching instructions for the skirt with extra flare.

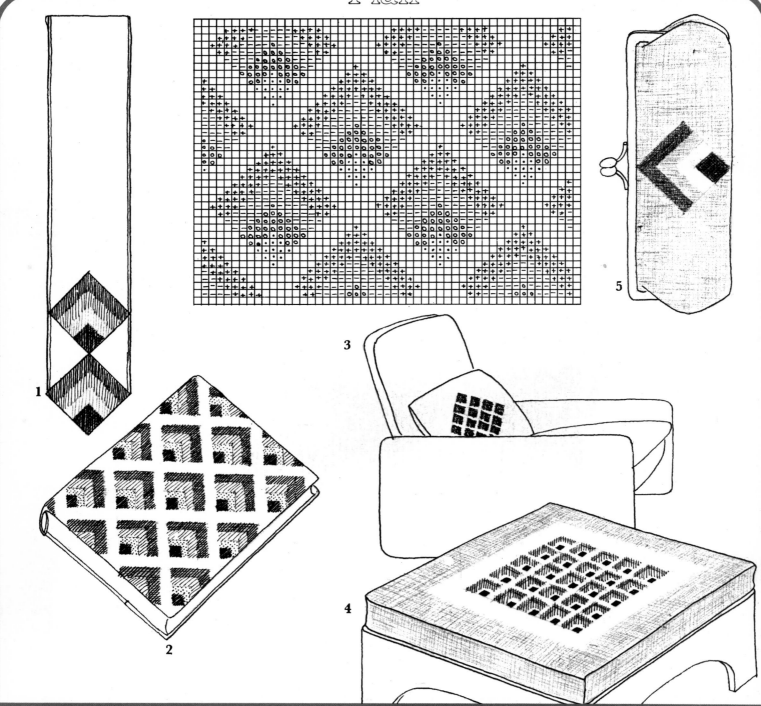

The effectiveness of modern embroidery is achieved by a combination of the subtle use of color, a variety of stitches and simple motifs.

This needlepoint design, based on a square, is an example of how a simple shape is made interesting by working parts of the design in toning colors or using stitches of different textures.

Art deco

1. *A matching bookmark gives an exclusive touch.*
2. *Personalize a diary or favorite book with an embroidered jacket cover.*
3. *Make a pillow to tone in with the color scheme of a room.*
4. *The repeated square on a box cushion adds to the clean symmetry of a modern stool.*
5. *Make a pretty purse for evening to match a favorite dress.*